"Our Constitut... ...rs. It serves as a great tool, insp... our democracy.

...David Eisner, President and CEO, National Constitution Center

"A timely and important explanation for America's young people!"

—Mrs. Laura W. Bush

"It is so encouraging to see young people like Juliette appreciate the great gift that is our Constitution and the freedoms that it guarantees."

—Jack Quinn, Former White House Counsel under President Bill Clinton

"Our Constitution Rocks is a fun, informative, and relevant book that will empower the youth in our country with the knowledge they need to succeed. Juliette Turner may be only 14 years old, but she highlights the importance of the Constitution for her generation and many to follow."

—Barbara Bush, Former First Lady of the United States

"Juliette's book is a great introduction to the Constitution and United States history for young people. It presents the events of our country's founding in a fun, easy-to-understand manner that kids and adults can enjoy alike. I look forward to sharing this book with my children and grandchildren."

—Congressman Dan Boren (D-OK)

"In this excellent book, Juliette Turner has a mission: to bridge the gap between the past and the present and to make the Constitution a living, breathing document for her contemporaries. By walking her reader though the words of the document, providing historical background, and then demonstrating how the Constitution still impacts their daily lives, she brings the past into the present and makes it fun too. Quite an accomplishment."

—Bruce Cole, a former Chairman of the National Endowment for the Humanities, is a Senior Fellow at the Hudson Institute.

"Our Constitution Rocks makes the brilliance of our Constitution and the founding principles of our country accessible to every young patriot."

—Congressman Scott Garrett (R-NJ),
Founder and Chairman of the Congressional Constitution Caucus

"Here is a great, fun way for young people to learn to understand, appreciate, respect, and love our Constitution."

—Myrna Blyth, Author of *How to Raise an American*

"It is always refreshing to see young people enthusiastic about the Constitution, and eager to spread the word. Juliette's effort to highlight the current relevance of the founding documents breathes fresh air into the cause of liberty."

—Michael Farris, Chancellor, Patrick Henry College;
Chairman and General Counsel, Home School Legal Defense Association

"So this is a great idea! A teenager writes a book explaining how the USA works for other teenagers. A very valuable tool for Am...

...y, Anchor, Fox News Channel

"This book not only informs, but it entertains and proves that learning about the Constitution goes way beyond the classroom! The greatest thing about this book is it's simplicity ... it's easy to understand, and all the while the reader is learning ... no matter what their age!"

—Leslie Marshall, Fox News Contributor,
Host of the nationally syndicated *The Leslie Marshall Show*

"*Our Constitution Rocks,* by Juliette Turner, is a fresh approach to teaching both history and constitutional principles. I am thrilled to have a young voice advocating these to her generation."

—Penny Nance, President and CEO, Concerned Women for America

"The Constitution is the foundation of our government and keeps it in check. *Our Constitution Rocks* teaches young people about the document and its importance to our country in an easy-to-understand format. Tea Party Patriots everywhere should pick up a copy!"

—Jenny Beth Martin, Tea Party Patriots Co-Founder and National Coordinator

"Juliette Turner's new book, *Our Constitution Rocks,* is the Constitution "made simple" for teens and kids everywhere. "

—Sonja Eddings Brown, Education Reformer and Founder of The Kitchen Cabinet

"The Constitution of the United States is a profound, timeless achievement. Yet it is neither complicated nor difficult to understand. It was written and ratified not for an elite class of specially trained people who would come to be known as "constitutional scholars," but for all of us as citizens. It is our Constitution. The type of government it establishes is, as President Lincoln said, government of, by, and for the people. But if self-government is to be sustained, if the republican form of government bequeathed to us by our Founding Fathers is to flourish, each generation of Americans must dedicate itself to understanding the Constitution. And that educational mission begins in the teen years, or even earlier. That's why I'm so pleased to see Juliette Turner's *Our Constitution Rocks.* Juliette presents key historical facts and constitutional principles in a clever and engaging way. Her fellow teens will learn from her book—and so will their parents."

—Robert P. George, McCormick Professor of Jurisprudence and Director of the
James Madison Program in American Ideals and Institutions, Princeton University

"As a father of five children, I am happy that Juliette has written this book to inspire young people to learn more about the United States Constitution. It is wonderful to see that a document over two hundred years old can still excite the imagination, hopefulness, and expectations of our nation's younger citizens in a way that bonds them both to our shared past and those values common to all Americans."

—Terry McAuliffe, Former Chairman of the Democratic National Committee

"George Washington and his fellow Founding Fathers acted to ensure that 'civil and religious liberty' would flourish in the new nation. Juliette Turner, one of the 'millions yet unborn' (in Washington's phrase) on whose behalf they acted, has written an energetic and precocious book to engage her fellow young people. Its argument—that the Founders accomplished something enduring and awesome—is vital. If the book is read with the energy with which it was written, it just might instill the kind of constitutional reverence we need to uphold our republic."

—Dr. Larry P. Arnn, President, Hillsdale College

OUR Constitution ROCKS!

"We the People" includes kids.

Written by **JULIETTE TURNER** National Youth Director Constituting America

Illustrations by Brian Oesch | Design by Ben Fetterley

ZONDERVAN®

ZONDERVAN.com/
AUTHORTRACKER
follow your favorite authors

To my mother, my best friend,
whose unwavering support and
love has made this possible.

We want to hear from you. Please send your comments about this
book to us in care of zreview@zondervan.com. Thank you.

ZONDERVAN

Our Constitution Rocks
Copyright © 2012 by Juliette Turner

Requests for information should be addressed to:

Zonderkidz, 5300 *Patterson Ave., S.E., Grand Rapids, Michigan 49530*

Library of Congress Cataloging-in-Publication Data

Turner, Juliette.
    Our constitution rocks / Juliette Turner.
        p. cm.
    Includes index.
    ISBN 978-0-310-73421-5
    1. Constitutional law — United States — Juvenile literature. [1. Constitutional law.] I. Title.
KF4550.Z9T87 2012
342.73—dc23   2012027889

Editor: Kim Childress
Cover design: Cindy Davis and Kris Nelson
Cover photography: Larry Travis Photography
Makeup artistry: Ro Vielma
Illustrations: Brian Oesch
Interior photography and illustrations: iStockphoto.com, ShutterStock.com
Interior design: Ben Fetterley and Sherri L. Hoffman

Printed in the United States of America

12 13 14 15 16 17 18 /DJM/ 29 28 27 26 25 24 23 22 21 20 19 18 17 16 15 14 13 12 11 10 9 8 7 6 5 4 3 2

CONTENTS

Acknowledgments
How my dream came true

This book is a true blessing in my life. What started out as a simple quest for knowledge about the Constitution has turned into a dream of a lifetime for a fourteen year old girl in Texas.

This book would not have been possible without, first and foremost, God. I thank Him for blessing me with this opportunity and for surrounding me with so many people who have stood with me in this process. Second of all, this whole project would not have been possible without my mother. Her love, dedication, and support through this process have been invaluable. Also, the vision for this book would not have occurred if not for her work in creating Constituting America. Without her, this book would not exist. Thank you, Mom.

I would also like to thank Cathy Gillespie, the co-chair of Constituting America, who is an ever faithful friend and fervent champion of the Constitution!

I also thank Kim Childress, the world's best editor and now my very good friend, who has given countless hours helping me polish and shape this book. She has been the champion of my book throughout this whole process through the halls of Zondervan. This book would not have been possible without her. From here, my gratitude goes to the Zondervan team who found interest in my compilation of ninety essays on the Constitution. I thank them for giving me the opportunity to spread the word about the Constitution through my book. I also would like to thank Victoria Ritter for her extraordinary efforts regarding research, along with Ben Fetterley and Sherri Hoffman, for adding such charm to the book with their captivating designs!

I also would like to thank my agent Rick Hersh, Peter Roff, and the many scholars from Constituting America who helped explain each line of the Constitution. I would especially like to thank the following scholars who gave of their time to help answer some of my question: Horace Cooper, Andrew Langer, and Professor Joerg Knipprath. I thank Professor Knipprath for his infinite knowledge on the Constitution, his unbelievable patience, and for spending so many hours with me over the phone making sure every word of the book was accurate.

Last but not least, without our Founding Fathers and their brilliant minds there would be no Constitution to explain. From the arguments between the Federalist and Anti-Federalists to the many relevant and timely quotes they stated way back then, all of these things are of priceless value to Americans today. I thank you Founding Fathers for giving us our country and the Constitution of the United States which forms our Republic. Be sure to check out the Constituting America website and the We The People 9.17 Contest for kids. Win prizes, a trip to Philadelphia and a starring role in a documentary. Categories include Best: Song, Short Film, Public Service Announcement, Essay, Drawing, or Poem. Go to www.constitutingamerica.org.

FOREWORD
The American Tree

Heritage is like a tree. You know, like the family tree. There's you, your mom and dad, your grandmother and grandfather, great-grandmother and great-grandfather, etc. Every generation lives within you and makes you who you are today: tall, short, blue eyes, brown, jolly, somber, graceful, or clumsy. All your characteristics are somehow aspects of your family tree. You wouldn't be you without the roots of your family.

The same can be said about the United States of America. The United States of America didn't just, poof, happen. We have an American tree. Our Founding Fathers and Mothers planted great ideas into the soil — life, liberty, and the pursuit of happiness — and gave them nutrients to flourish — checks and balances of power and the peoples' voice and votes.

The American Tree has been growing for over 236 years, since the Declaration of Independence. Your family heritage has been the guardians, or the gardeners, of the American Tree. The collective genius and dedication of the American people has kept it alive.

The American Tree is easily injured. You must protect the American Tree from storms, or tyranny, which is a cruel use of power by a man, or a government that restricts speech, religious beliefs, and freedom to seek one's own path in life.

Our Founding Fathers experienced these cruel acts and restraints. So they declared independence from the tyrant king. They declared something new—that God had given men and women their natural born rights—life, liberty, and the pursuit of happiness — not a person or a government —but God. Think about it: if government gives you rights, then government can take them away. If God gives you your rights, then no person or government can take them away. What amazing, new seeds our Founding Fathers planted for the American Tree.

Tyranny existed 236 years ago, and tyranny still exists today. The American Tree's freedom to prosper is not guaranteed. It has to be protected by you. You do this with knowledge. Knowledge is power. These nutrients of power are in a type of gardener's guidebook — the United States Constitution. It has seven Articles and twenty-seven Amendments.

Join Juliette in her mission to preserve, protect, and defend the American Tree. Learn your guidebook. In your hands, in your wisdom, in your dedication, lay the liberties, vitality, and future of the United States of America.

Janine Turner, Juliette's mom,
Founder and Co-Chair of Constituting America

INTRODUCTION

In 1787, a group of men gathered to create the shortest Constitution in the history of the world: the Constitution of the United States of America. Yet, why would this matter to my generation, today, 225 years later? America is very different today than it was in our Founding Fathers' era. Facebook has replaced the Pony Express, Apple iPads have replaced the quill pen and parchment, the hybrid automobile has replaced the horse and buggy, xbox has replaced the corn husk doll, and to say the least, our Founding Fathers would faint at the sight of a 700,000 pound "metal bird" in the sky.

In fact, what if Mark Zuckerberg was imprisoned for creating Facebook? What if you and your family could be persecuted for Twittering your thoughts? You don't like your parents saying you can't see a certain movie, right? What if you lived in a country where people were imprisoned for creating or watching a certain type of movie? You like being able to express yourself with the type of clothes you wear, right? What if the government made us all dress a certain way?

Kids like me ask, "Why should I care about some old document written by a bunch of old guys in wigs and stockings?" You may think you have more important things to worry about. Well, I'm here to tell you that you should care as much about our Constitution as you do about your Facebook status.

This could be reality if not for the Constitution. The Founding Fathers created our constitution so people today can speak out, own property, worship God, attend youth group, and much more.

Not only does the Constitution forever protect our rights, it establishes our republican form of government, where the people rule through their representatives; a government in which the power belongs to the people through their right to vote. The Constitution, in Articles One, Two, and Three, gives us our legislative, executive, and judicial branches of government. It establishes a system of checks and balances that prevent America from being ruled by a dictator. Our Bill of Rights forever protects our rights to live and pursue our dreams. Because of the Constitution, we don't have to worry that when we wake up in the morning, all the rules will have changed.

The Framers knew our Constitution would need to be amended, so they included a perfect plan for the Constitution to be changed — not too easy, which would allow corruptions, and not too hard, so that the people could change it.

Three years ago, at age eleven, my mother read the entire Constitution to me while sitting in our hammock, over my spring break. Before then, I had heard about the Constitution, but I didn't know it. It is so important for my generation, and future generations, to gain a deeper understanding of the document that makes America the greatest nation on earth. Our Constitution survives because of "We the People." If we neglect the foundation of our country, our freedoms will slowly crumble from under our feet. It is up to us to rally around the Constitution and preserve it.

As National Youth Director of Constituting America, I was inspired to learn more, thus I wrote ninety essays on the Constitution. This event planted the seed which grew into the creation of this book. I wrote this book to give my generation a fun way to learn about the Constitution.

A woman once asked Benjamin Franklin after the completion of the Constitution, "Sir, what form of government have you given us?" Franklin replied, "A Republic, ma'am, if you can keep it."

"List the constitutional amendments in any order? Hmm...4th, 10th... umm...6th, 8th, 5th ..."

BENJAMIN FRANKLIN

A Republic, ma'am, if you can keep it.

I want to Keep it. Don't you?

HOW TO READ THIS BOOK

Since I am a teenager like you, I accept and understand that our attention span is about five seconds, so I've broken down the information into sections:

The Bottom Line
A simplified, understandable, plain-English version of what each section is about.

What Were They Thinking?
Why the Framers thought this particular aspect of the Constitution was important.

Why Should I Care?
How the information affects us today in our lives and in the future.

Breakin' it Down
This explains what the article or clause means in more detail, including context (what was going on at the time).

How Can I Make a Difference?
Tells you, the reader, how you can use the knowledge you just learned and make a difference!

What Has It Done For Me Lately?
This fun fact will tell you a modern day example of how the Constitution is working in our lives.

Fun Facts
Lots of fun tidbits, including:

FOUNDING Father Forum

★ Interesting tidbits on our Founding Fathers, regular men who ended up shaping our nation.

Convention Chat
Stuff you probably don't know about the Constitutional Convention and how it came to be (the meeting where everyone got together and wrote the Constitution).

COLONIAL Compare and Contrast
Charts to help you distinguish one great idea from another.

Pop Quiz! and By the way (BTW): Random fun facts that might appear anywhere on the page.

OUR BRITISH ROOTS
Why our Founding Fathers wanted to do things in regard to Britain.

Quotes from our Founding Fathers and other interesting folks.

JAMES MADISON

ARTICLE Action
Bringing it back to the Articles of Confederation and why it was changed.

AMENDMENT Preview
A sneak peak at changes to come.

Real arguments about each idea, illustrated documentary style, with commentary by Juliette.

LIBERTY Language
Constitution Vocabulary: Words you should know but probably won't use in daily conversation.

GEORGE WASHINGTON

The Signing of the Constitution of the United States, by Howard Chandler Christy

Pop Quiz! Do you know who all these people are? Go to page 221 to find out.

PROLOGUE
The Articles of Confederation

*Decades leading to the Constitutional Convention
in a few short paragraphs*

By Kim Childress

After the Revolutionary War ended in 1783, the thirteen states had won their freedom, but they were definitely not united. America had adopted a system of government under "The Articles of Confederation," which technically formed our first Constitution, but actually had lots of problems. After the Revolutionary War, the Articles of Confederation set up rules each state agreed to follow, but they didn't. Congress would ask states to contribute money for the country's debts, but the states wouldn't pay. Congress needed legislators from each state to rule in Congress, but the states wouldn't send representatives. Congress could declare war, but the states could refuse to send soldiers—and Congress couldn't do anything about it.

Under the Articles of Confederation, the central government was weak. Each state thought of itself as its own little country. We had no Union. America needed help.

To address the problems, in 1787, Congress told the states to send delegates to Philadelphia, with instructions to revise the Articles of Confederation. Fifty-five representatives from twelve of the thirteen states debated the pros and cons of the current government—Rhode Island refused to send anyone. These

Convention Chat

The "Grand Convention" later became known as the Constitutional Convention. Twelve states sent delegates to Philadelphia to revise and improve the Articles of Confederation. George Washington, Alexander Hamilton, and James Madison were a few of those men.

... seven states needed to be present, so the convention didn't start until May 25th.

BTW: The Constitutional Convention was supposed to start on May 14, 1787, but most of the delegates were late. Representatives from at least

Convention Chat

James Madison and George Washington were the first Framers to show up.

It is impossible to consider the degree of concord which ultimately prevailed less than a miracle.

In other words, it was a miracle that they all agreed long enough to create the Constitution.

men soon realized they had a mighty task before them. They were going to have to draft something completely new, a Republic, a system of government where the people ruled.

Our Founding Fathers examined previous governments to see what had worked, and they found, "No existing government was designed to provide its people with freedom, prosperity, and peace." Our Founding Fathers wanted absolute freedom, they wanted the states to be united, and they wanted the people to have unalienable rights. The Framers wanted a government with checks and balances that didn't prohibit the people. They had to find a perfect formula for freedom — a balance between a democracy and a republic.

JAMES MADISON

What these great men were proposing was unheard of! It was crazy, revolutionary, and dangerous. While they debated, they swore themselves to secrecy and managed to keep their silence for four long months. At the end of that unforgettable period of our nation's history, our Founding Fathers established a nearly perfect formula for freedom, the first ever of its kind, in the whole world! And then they all agreed on it! These great thinkers united our nation under the Constitution, which has endured for 225 years, making it the oldest, operative, written constitution in the history of the world.

FOUNDING Father Forum

★ James Madison was a great historian who studied past governments, and he was the main author of our current Constitution. During the debates, Madison wrote down all that was said.

Convention Chat

Once they realized the huge task before them, the delegates agreed to keep the debates a secret because they didn't want people listening in and taking sides. Fifty-five men managed to keep their proceedings private for four months!

FOUNDING Father Forum

★ George Washington was elected president of the convention.

FOUNDING Father Forum

★ Benjamin Franklin arrived to the convention in a sedan chair carried by four prisoners from the Philadelphia jail. He was eighty-one years old and had a hard time walking.

BTW: all of the states sent delegates to the Constitutional Convention except for Rhode Island (or as George Washington called it, "Rogue Island").

COLONIAL Compare and Contrast

Founding Fathers versus Framers

Founding Fathers, or Founders, refers to the political leaders of the struggle for American independence against Britain, including the leaders in the Revolutionary War, the signers of the Declaration of Independence, and also the Framers of the Constitution. The Framers of the Constitution, or Framers, were men who debated and wrote the Constitution. So all the Framers were Founders, but not all the Founders were Framers. Thomas Jefferson, for example, was not involved in the drafting of the Constitution because he was in France representing the new United States as administer. So Jefferson was a Founder but not a Framer. Some other Founders include George Washington, Benjamin Franklin, Alexander Hamilton, John Adams, James Madison, and Patrick Henry.

Where the framers of the Constitution bought their frames.

www.CartoonStock.com

15

Debate

After an unequivocal experience of the inefficacy of the subsisting federal government, you are called upon to deliberate on a new Constitution for the United States of America.

At the time, people were very excited about the proposed Constitution. Redick was worried people were all hyped up to ratify the Constitution without really looking at it first.

There are material imperfections in our national system, and something is necessary to be done to rescue us from impending anarchy.

In my opinion the day on which we adopt the present proposed plan of government, from that moment we may justly date the loss of American liberty.

He's saying that there are major problems with the current system, and if something isn't done, the Union will fall apart.

ALEXANDER HAMILTON

DAVID REDICK

The subject speaks its own importance; comprehending in its consequences nothing less than the existence of the UNION, the safety and welfare of the parts of which it is composed, the fate of an empire in many respects the most interesting in the world.

I hope Congress will be very deliberate and digest it thoroughly before they send it recommended to the states. I sincerely hope that such Gentlemen as were members of convention, and who have seats in Congress may not be considered as very proper judges of their own works.

I pray a spirit of wisdom and a spirit of integrity pervade Congress, more especially at this time.

ALEXANDER HAMILTON

DAVID REDICK

He's saying that Congress better seriously think before sending the Constitution out for approval, and it's not fair if the same guys who wrote the Constitution get to vote on it.

It seems to have been reserved to the people of this country, by their conduct and example, to decide the important question, whether societies of men are really capable or not of establishing good government from reflection and choice, or whether they are forever destined to depend for their political constitutions on accident and force. If there be any truth in the remark, the crisis at which we are arrived may with propriety be regarded as the era in which that decision is to be made; and a wrong election of the part we shall act may, in this view, deserve to be considered as the general misfortune of mankind.

— ALEXANDER HAMILTON

The outcome of what happens is hugely important, and the rest of the world is watching to see what happens next.

THE PREAMBLE

to the United States Constitution

We the People of the United States, in Order to form a more perfect Union, establish Justice, insure domestic Tranquility, provide for the common defence, promote the general Welfare, and secure the Blessings of Liberty to ourselves and our Posterity, do ordain and establish this Constitution for the United States of America.

FOUNDING Father Forum

★ The Preamble was composed by Pennsylvanian Gouverneur Morris, who was extremely talkative and among the most profound of all the delegates.

The Bottom Line

This short paragraph sums up what the Constitution – and the government it created – is meant to accomplish. It is *not law*! It is simply an introduction.

What Were They Thinking?

Gouverneur Morris wrote this small yet brilliantly composed paragraph to clarify what the Constitution was intended to accomplish.

Why Should I Care?

The Preamble sums up who we are and what we stand for as a country.

Breakin' It Down

We the People of the United States: At this time, the use of the words "We the People" was revolutionary and had never been heard before. The Articles of Confederation had been an agreement among the states, but according to this new phrase, the Constitution had everything to do with the people.

To form a more perfect Union: The goal of the Constitution is to unify the states in areas such as commerce, national security, and currency, so that the nation can prosper and be safe.

Establish Justice, insure domestic Tranquility, provide for the common defense: This phrase is an example of the government's job and what it was intended to do.

Promote the general welfare: The government is to promote, not provide, the conditions for a life of freedom. The Anti-Federalists, or those against the Constitution, thought this phrase would grant the government too much power. It turns out, the Anti-Federalists were somewhat correct. Today, this phrase

Convention Chat

The Preamble was the last element added to the Constitution at the Constitutional Convention.

ARTICLE Action

Originally, the Constitutional Convention was only intended to revise critical issues within the Articles of Confederation.

is used to fund certain projects that might benefit members of Congress or some "favorite" constituents rather than the people as a whole.

Secure the Blessings of Liberty to ourselves and our Posterity: The Constitution was written to limit our government's power so that the liberties of the people will always be protected.

How Can I Make a Difference?

Memorize the Preamble and its true meaning and then share it with your friends.

What Has It Done For Me Lately?

The Preamble reminds us daily of our patriotic duty as a country to uphold our Constitution! Learn more about it at the Constitution Center online, at www.constitutioncenter.org.

COLONIAL Compare and Contrast
Anti-Federalists v. Federalists

Anti-Federalists: A group of people who opposed the adoption of the U.S. Constitution.

Federalists: Advocates of a federal Union between the American colonies after the revolution and of the adoption of the U.S. Constitution, favoring a strong, centralized, national government.

Convention Chat

Did "the People" really establish the Constitution? Yes and no. The delegates selected to draft the Constitution in 1787 were chosen by state legislatures, not by general election (by the people), but before it was ratified, the Constitution had to be approved by the people in each state.

FOUNDING Father Forum

★ At the conclusion of the Constitutional Convention, Benjamin Franklin observed the symbol of a half-sun on George Washington's chair and remarked, "I have the happiness to know that it is a rising and not a setting sun."

LIBERTY Language

Constitution: The basic principles and laws of a nation, state, or social group that determine the powers and duties of the government and guarantee certain rights to the people in it.

Preamble: An introductory statement.

Convention Chat

It took one hundred days to actually "frame" the Constitution.

Portrait by Rembrandt Peale

We hold these truths to be self-evident, that all men are created equal, that they are endowed by their Creator with certain unalienable Rights, that among these are Life, Liberty, and the pursuit of Happiness.

—Declaration of Independence

— THOMAS JEFFERSON

Debate

Back then, each state thought of itself as its own country.

I have the highest veneration of those gentlemen — but sir, give me leave to demand, what right had they to say, "We, the People"? My political curiosity, exclusive of my anxious solicitude for the public welfare, leads me to ask who authorized them to speak the language of, "We, the People," instead of "We, the States"? States are the characteristics, and the soul of the confederation. If the states be not the agents of this compact, it must be one of great consolidated national government of the people of all the states.

Two sovereignties cannot co-exist within the same limits. Giving powers to Congress must eventuate in a bad government or in no government.

The thirteen states are thirteen Sovereign bodies.

PATRICK HENRY

OLIVER ELLSWORTH

ALEXANDER HAMILTON

SETTING UP THE CONGRESS
ARTICLE I
Section 1

All legislative Powers herein granted shall be vested in a Congress of the United States which shall consist of a Senate and House of Representatives.

FOUNDING Father Forum

★ James Madison is known as the father of our Constitution.

BTW: Article I is the longest article in the Constitution and is all about Congress!

> Where there is no law there is no freedom.

JOHN LOCKE

The Bottom Line

Article I Section 1 describes how the legislative branch is broken down into two separate branches – a bicameral legislature made up of the House and Senate.

What Were They Thinking?

Our Founding Fathers knew that the current government under the Articles of Confederation needed to be changed. James Madison wanted to form a new structure of government that would have three different branches, who would constantly be checking each other. One of these branches would be a bicameral legislature with the House and Senate.

Why Should I Care?

The Congress and Congressional officials represent you in Washington, D.C. Have you ever heard someone tell you to "contact your representative in Washington"? Well, thanks to our Founding Fathers and Article I, Section 1, we have people in Washington, D.C. who are, or are supposed to be, listening to our needs.

Breakin' It Down

This is how the plan for our legislative branch came about. While waiting for the other delegates to arrive at the Convention, James Madison etched out the Virginia Plan, where he wrote about his plan for the government.

> The accumulation of all powers, legislative, executive and judiciary, in the same hands, whether of one, a few, or many, and whether hereditary, self-appointed, or elective, may justly be pronounced the very definition of tyranny.

JAMES MADISON

The first and most important branch of any government was the Legislature, for that branch represents the people.

JOHN LOCKE

He felt that the Articles of Confederation needed to be trashed and that the thirteen separated states needed to be merged into one united country. He also planned for there to be a bicameral legislature, but the number of delegates per state would be based on the state's financial contributions or the state's populace. He established the three-branch system of government, as well. Governor Edmund Randolph then introduced this plan on behalf of James Madison to their fellow delegates on May 29, 1787. It did not sit well with the delegates from Delaware and New Hampshire, the smaller states. These delegates were unhappy because smaller states wouldn't have as many delegates as larger states. In response, the smaller states introduced the New Jersey plan, which focused on equal representation for all states in the legislature.

This argument led to the Connecticut Compromise, or the Great Compromise of July 29, 1787. This compromise accepted the plan of having a bicameral legislature, yet, in one branch the number of delegates would be based on population – the House – and the other branch would have an equal amount of delegates per state – the Senate.

OUR BRITISH ROOTS

Congress, under the Articles of Confederation, was a unicameral legislature. So where did our Founding Fathers get this idea for a bicameral legislature? Some came partially from the writings of the British Constitution, which the delegates had admired.

LIBERTY Language

Bicameral Legislature: A governmental body with two houses or chambers, such as the US Congress or British Parliament.

Debate

Read the actual words spoken by our Framers.

> There was no more reason that a great individual state contributing much should have more votes than a small one contributing little, than that a rich individual citizen should have more votes than an indigent one.

WILLIAM PATERSON

> Back then, you had to be a landowner in order to vote, and he is arguing that this is wrong. It shouldn't matter how rich or poor, everyone's vote should be equal. In the same way, larger states shouldn't have more votes than smaller states.

Today, since the House contains more representatives per state, their job is to listen to the peoples' needs and desires. The Senate's job is to represent the states, balancing the passions of the people.

How Can I Make a Difference?
Make sure your elected official in Congress is doing his job: representing you in Washington, D.C. Google their voting record!

What Has It Done For Me Lately?
This section is still in effect today! Our Congress is still made up of a Senate and a House of Representatives who are constantly performing their jobs of passing legislation, debating legislation, and constantly checking each other's actions.

FOUNDING Father Forum
★ James Madison reviewed all past republics that had failed, in order not to repeat their mistakes.

FOUNDING Father Forum
★ James Madison found it important to have a written Constitution. France, who ended up in horrible bloodshed and under a ruthless dictator Napoleon, had a written constitution, but it did not have the same checks and balances that our Founding Fathers included in our Constitution.

ARTICLE I
Section 2

Clauses 1–2

[1]*The House of Representatives shall be composed of Members chosen every second Year by the People of the several States, and the Electors in each State shall have the Qualifications requisite for Electors of the most numerous Branch of the State Legislature.*

[2]*No Person shall be a Representative who shall not have attained to the Age of twenty five Years, and been seven Years a Citizen of the United States, and who shall not, when elected, be an Inhabitant of that State in which he shall be chosen.*

The Bottom Line

Article I, Section 2, Clauses 1–2 sum up the requirements for being a representative in the House, who gets to vote, and how often Representatives are elected.

What Were They Thinking?

Our Founding Fathers put very serious thought into who could run for office, and they established that Congressional elections be held every second year, so that our representatives must listen to the needs and wants of "We the People."

FOUNDING Father Forum

★ Our Founders might have chosen seven years as a requirement to become a representative, because at the time they wrote the Constitution, our country was still very young, and most of our population was made up of immigrants.

Why Should I Care?

If you ever wanted to run for Congress, you need to know the rules and requirements. Also, without this clause, there would be no check on who could run for Congress. What if a sixteen-year-old ran for Congress? Think about it!

Breakin' It Down

The House is the larger of the two Congressional branches. The number of representatives for each state is determined by population, and House elections are held every two years.

Our Founding Fathers pondered deeply the decision of how frequently federal elections would take place. Since our representatives are up for election every second year, they have to be accountable to the people they represent. If the elections were more frequent, there is a risk that House members would stay in perpetual election mode—constantly campaigning. If the elections were held less frequently, the House members might abuse their positions. The two-year cycle provides a happy medium, ensuring accountability while letting House members do their job.

How Can I Make a Difference?

Find out more about your representative in the House: find out their age, when they first entered politics, what bills and legislation they have proposed, and on which committees they serve. Learn all this and more at www.house.gov.

What Has It Done For Me Lately?

Today, a representative has to be living in the state he or she will be representing at the time of the election. But the Constitution never specifies that the representative has to be a resident of his or her county or district. The issue of living in your county or district is still being debated today.

★ ARTICLE Action

Under the Articles of Confederation, representatives were elected every year. This was too short, because members were constantly campaigning and didn't have enough time to work!

"You're wrong. Today 12 thumbs-up on Facebook IS a mandate for me to run for Congress!"

www.CartoonStock.com

FOUNDING Father Forum

★ To be a representative, our Founding Fathers thought that a twenty-five-year-old was mature enough to perform wisely and influence the political process within his generation.

FOUNDING Father Forum

★ In our Founding Fathers' day, rules for voting were different across the country and determined by each state, so whatever the rules were for a person to vote in a state House election became the same rules for voting in the federal House election. Today voting rules are the same for everyone — you must be 18 and registered.

JAMES MADISON

The greater the power is, the shorter ought to be its duration.

ARTICLE I
Section 2

Clause 3

Representatives and direct Taxes shall be apportioned among the several States which may be included within this Union, according to their respective Numbers, which shall be determined by adding to the whole Number of free Persons, including those bound to Service for a Term of Years, and excluding Indians not taxed, three fifths of all other Persons.

The Bottom Line

Article I, Section 2, Clause 3 is best known as the Three-Fifths Clause. It says the number of representatives in the House will be based on the population of each state. At the time, the total population for each state meant the number of free people, plus the number of indentured servants, and three-fifths of "all other people." In other words, three-fifths of slaves.

What Were They Thinking?

Our Founding Fathers had to figure a way to determine taxes and the number of Representatives needed for each state. Basing representation on population brought up the issue of slavery because the southern states had more slaves, and therefore more people, more representatives, and more sway in Congress. Though many of our Framers were against slavery, they knew a compromise was needed to get the south to accept the Constitution, resulting in the Three-Fifths Clause.

FOUNDING Father Forum

★ Our Founding Fathers knew they couldn't tackle the issue of slavery at that time, because if they did, the southern states would never have voted in favor of the Constitution.

Why Should I Care?

This clause was changed by two amendments in the Constitution. So why do we need to know about it? I'll tell you why! Even though the "three-fifths" portion of the clause was amended, our House of Representatives is still based on state population, which is what this clause established.

Breakin' It Down

This clause is known as the Three-Fifths Clause, and it established a method for calculating how much each state would pay in taxes and how many representatives per state by adding the number of free people, indentured servants and three-fifths of slaves.

The "three-fifths" clause was a compromise. Without it, the Union would have dissolved! Slaves being counted as "three-fifths" was a sad part of our history; however, between 1776 and 1787, there were approximately 10,000 free African-Americans who were included in the "whole number of free persons" category.

ARTICLE Action

This clause originated from the language of the Articles of Confederation. Their first idea was to base representation on land value, but back then it was extremely difficult and tedious to survey land. Scratch that off! So instead, they based the number of representatives for each state on its population.

Convention Chat

The idea of a population-based Congress nearly ended the Constitution discussions. The only way to move forward was to compromise.

AMENDMENT Preview

Fortunately, this particular clause was amended two different times: Amendment 14 and Amendment 26. Amendment 14 took away the "three-fifths" clause and made the voting age twenty-one. Amendment 26 changed the voting age to eighteen.

For when you assemble a number of men to have the advantage of their joint wisdom, you inevitably assemble with those men, all their prejudices, their passions, their errors of opinion, their local interests, and their selfish views. From such an assembly can a perfect production be expected? It therefore astonishes me, Sir, to find this system approaching so near to perfection as it does.

BENJAMIN FRANKLIN

Debate

I urge strenuously that express security ought to be provided for including slaves in the ratio of Representation. I lament that such a species of property exists. But as it did exist, the holders of such properties would require this security. It was perceived that the design was entertained by some of excluding slaves altogether; the Legislature therefore ought not to be left at liberty.

The rule of contribution by direct taxation for the support of the Government of the U. States shall be the number of white inhabitants, and three-fifths of every other description in the several States, until some other rule that shall more accurately ascertain the wealth of the several States can be devised and adopted by the Legislature.

Every individual of the community at large has an equal right to the protection of government.

Randolph was saying he thought slaves should also have representation, and he was upset at the idea of slaves being considered "property." A lot of the Founding Fathers were against slavery, but they knew they couldn't tackle the issue at that time, because then southern states would never have voted in favor of the Constitution.

OLIVER ELLSWORTH

ALEXANDER HAMILTON

EDMUND RANDOLPH

How Can I Make a Difference?

Research how many representatives your state has in the House and to which Congressional district you belong. Find your congressmen at www.house.gov.

What Has It Done For Me Lately?

If your state recently had a change in population, then your state may have been redistricted. State officials redistrict to figure out if more or less representatives are needed in Washington, D.C., to represent your state.

Districts/Redistricting: Districts are decided according to the population of an area, which in turn is determined by a *census* – a population survey. The national census takes place every ten years; the last one occurred in 2010. From here, the process gets tricky. The national congressional districts and the state legislative districts have to be established. It is very important that the border lines are drawn to encompass the same amount of people so they may have a fair share in the way they are governed. Each state has differing criteria for deciding the district boundaries, as long as they comply with the federal regulations. Since the last census occurred only a couple years ago, many states are still in the process of redistricting. Right now, the state of New York is undergoing a very long redistricting process.

WORDS OF WISDOM

The Framers of the Constitution knew human nature as well as we do. They too had lived in dangerous days; they too knew the suffocating influence of orthodoxy and standardized thought. They weighed the compulsions for restrained speech and thought against the abuses of liberty. They chose liberty.

—Justice William O. Douglas

wikimedia.com, public domain

ARTICLE I
Section 2

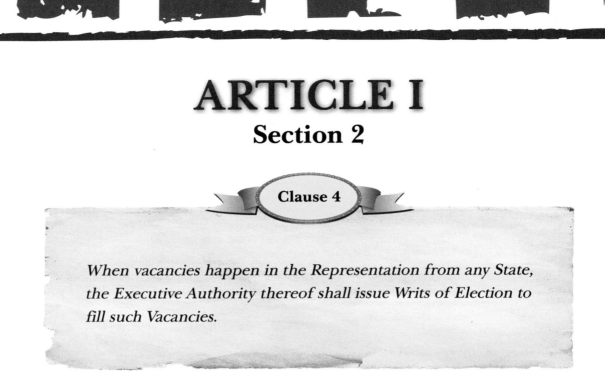

Clause 4

When vacancies happen in the Representation from any State, the Executive Authority thereof shall issue Writs of Election to fill such Vacancies.

The Bottom Line
Article I, Section 2, Clause 4 establishes that when a representative resigns from office, the governor of the state calls for a special election to fill the resigning representative's seat in the House.

What Were They Thinking?
Our Founding Fathers wanted to ensure the people were represented—always. It is also interesting that our Founders wanted the *states* to have the power to fill vacancies, *not* the national government.

Why Should I Care?
Wouldn't you be kind of miffed if you found out your representative in the U.S. House had resigned, and you no longer had representation in Washington, D.C.? This could be a problem. Take, for example, if the House was voting on a bill

to mandate that everyone must drive the same kind of car in your state. If your representative had resigned, then you wouldn't have anyone to represent your voice in the vote! Thankfully this scenario will never happen because of Article I, Section 2, Clause 4.

Breakin' It Down
The phrase "...the Executive Authority thereof shall issue Writs of Election..." means that the executive authority of that state (the governor) has the power and the responsibility to call for an election to fill the vacancy.

How Can I Make a Difference?
Find out how many times your state governor has had to organize special elections to fill a vacant spot in the U.S. House. See if there was ever a time when your representative resigned, and a special election was held in your district.

OUR BRITISH ROOTS

The issue of filling vacancies came up in our Founding Father's time period when William Pinkney, a representative from Maryland, resigned from the House. In Britain's House of Commons, resignation was not allowed. Our Founding Fathers felt if a representative wanted to resign, he or she should be allowed to do so.

What Has It Done For Me Lately?
A recent example is the resignation of Representative Gabrielle Giffords (D–AZ). Rep. Giffords was shot and severely wounded during a local event in January 2011. After a year of recovery, Giffords decided to resign. Arizona Governor Jan Brewer announced that she would call a special election for the state's 8th Congressional District seat.

BTW: This authority was granted to the STATE governor, not an executive on the FEDERAL level.

Pop Quiz! Do you know the difference?

ARTICLE I
Section 2

Clause 5

The House of Representatives shall chuse the Speaker and other Officers; and shall have the sole Power of Impeachment.

The Bottom Line

Article I, Section 2, Clause 5 grants the House the ability to choose their speaker (the leader of the House), and it also gives the House a very important responsibility—the power of impeachment.

What Were They Thinking?

Our Founding Fathers wanted the House to have a leader that they respected, a leader that they would listen to. They also wanted to give the House, the people's house, the sole power to impeach federal officers.

Why Should I Care?

Impeachment is very serious. When you vote, you want to keep in mind that the person you elect into office can possibly decide whether or not to impeach another official, even the president! This responsibility is huge, and you don't want it falling into the hands of the wrong people.

Pop Quiz! Can you think of a reason why the Framers gave this power to the House?

Breakin' It Down

BTW: Notice the misspelling of the word chuse in Clause 5. The Constitution has lots of mistakes. To find out why, check out the info on page 40.

Our Founding Fathers specifically gave the House authority to choose their own speaker, or leader. This ensures the House leader will be respected by the House majority, and he or she will lead effectively. This power could have been given to the president or the Electoral College.

This clause also grants the power of impeachment to the federal House of Representatives. *However*, the House may have the power to call for an impeachment, but the trial of the person being impeached takes place on the Senate floor. *And* if the president is the official being impeached, the Chief Justice of the U. S. Supreme Court will preside over the trial. Otherwise, the vice president will preside over the trial. This method involves all three branches of government—an example of the importance of checks and balances.

LIBERTY Language

Impeachment: The removal of a governmental official due to an offense.

How Can I Make a Difference?

Find out who is the current Speaker of the House at www.speaker.gov. What state is he or she from, and how long has he or she served in Congress?

What Has It Done For Me Lately?

After the 2010 congressional elections, Representative Nancy Pelosi (D-CA) handed over her position as Speaker to Representative John Boehner (R-OH). Before the election of 2010, and for the first time in many years, the speaker was a Democrat, the president was a Democrat, and the house majority was Democratic. A lot more liberal policies could get passed because everyone was in agreement. However, the people, in 2010, became dissatisfied because unemployment was high, the country was in a recession, and the new policies hadn't improved conditions enough. The people "spoke" their dissatisfaction by voting in a new Republican majority in the House of Representatives, which led to the election of a Republican speaker.

ARTICLE Action

Under the Articles of Confederation, our three federal powers – legislative, executive, and judicial – were combined into one body, the Congress. Today, under the Constitution, only the legislative branch resides in the Congress; all three branches – legislative, executive, and judicial – are separated. Our Founding Fathers feared if one person presided over one branch, like the system set up under the Articles of Confederation, that person could become a tyrant. So our Founders created a three-branch system of government with checks and balances.

ARTICLE I
Section 3

The Senate of the United States shall be composed of two Senators from each State, chosen by the Legislature thereof, for six Years; and each Senator shall have one Vote.

The Bottom Line

Article I, Section 3, Clause 1 established every state would have two senators, each with one vote; they were to be elected by their state legislatures and up for re-election every six years.

What Were They Thinking?

Our Founding Fathers wanted both the people and the states to be represented in the Republican form of government they were creating. The House of Representatives was considered "the voice of the people," and the Senate was considered the "voice of the states."

Convention Chat

The debate between small-state and large-state delegates consumed more time and energy than any other item discussed during the Constitutional Convention.

FOUNDING Father Forum

★ Gouverneur Morris also agreed with the plan of a bicameral legislature, but he thought that the Senate should represent the merchants, financiers, and gentlemen, and the House should represent the middle class and farmers.

Why Should I Care?

The Senate is the second branch of our bicameral legislature and provides a check on the House of Representatives. It's important to have a check on the House so they can't get away with passing a bill that would take away some of our freedoms.

Breakin' It Down

Article I, Section 2 lays out the laws for the House of Representatives. Article I, Section 3 lays out the laws for the Senate.

Who was to choose the members of the Senate? The house was already representing the people, chosen by the people. If senators were chosen by members of the House, the Senate would closely resemble the House's views. So our Founding Fathers decided that the state legislatures would elect the federal Senate. (This was later changed by Amendment 17.)

With the Senate representing the states, a new question arose — wouldn't larger states overpower smaller ones? This is why our Founders established two senators per state, and one vote per senator. Our Founders thought senators could be elected every six years because they were to represent the states, not the "passions of the people."

How Can I Make a Difference?

Do you know the two senators from your state? If not, find out at www.senate.gov. Take it even further by finding out their voting record. Have they been present for votes? Have they refused to vote on legislation passed by the House?

What Has It Done For Me Lately?

Find out more about a bill that has been passed by the House but not by the Senate.

Pop Quiz! Remember the Connecticut Compromise?

BTW: The "new form of government" proposed by our Founding Fathers gave the average person, not only kings and queens, the ability to own their own property and reap the benefits of their land.

★ ★

Misspellings in the US Constitution

Notice the spelling errors throughout the Constitution? Were our Founding Fathers geniuses who couldn't spell?

Actually, the Constitution was written in 1787 in the manner of the day — in other words, it was written by hand. According to the National Archives, the version we are most familiar with today was penned by Jacob Shallus, a clerk for the Pennsylvania State Assembly. In the document itself are several words which are misspelled. Back then they didn't have spell checkers and easy edits, so these misspellings survive in the document today.

One glaring mistake is the word "Pennsylvania" in the list of participants, spelled with a single "N," *Pensylvania*. Previously, in Article I, Section 2, it was spelled with two. However, the single "N" was common usage in the 18th century — the Liberty Bell, for example, has the single "N" spelling inscribed upon it.

Another mistake, though less obvious, is a common one even today: the word "it's" is used in Article I, Section 10, but the word "its" should have been used.

The most common mistake, at least to modern eyes, is the word "choose," spelled "chuse" several times. This is less a mistake than it is an alternate spelling used at the time. The word is found in the Constitution as both "chuse" and "chusing."

Other misspellings include "defence," "controul," and "labour." Most of the misspellings are in the original document, which was written hastily after the Convention concluded. However, besides one use of British spelling in the Bill of Rights ("defence" in the 6th), the amendments are all error-free, because the writers had more time to proofread and the benefit of a standardized American dictionary.

What Gouverneur Morris is saying is that the idea of "mutual check and security" was spot on, but not the idea of separate branches of Congress representing separate classes of people.

The Senate ought to represent the interests of the oligarchies consisting of urban merchants and financiers as well as country gentlemen. The house ought to represent everyone else, particularly the middling classes of small farmers and shopkeepers. The two forces will controul each other, providing a mutual check and a mutual security.

GOUVERNEUR MORRIS

The senators would represent no particular class or caste; they would represent the constituent states of the United States. Without titles of nobility or any set level of wealth, the Senators as such would have no interests separate from those of the people.

It is ESSENTIAL to such a government that it be derived from the great body of the society, not from an inconsiderable proportion, or a favored class of it; otherwise a handful of tyrannical nobles, exercising their oppressions by a delegation of their powers, might aspire to the rank of republicans, and claim for their government the honorable title of republic ... The House of Representatives will derive its powers from the people of America; ... The Senate, on the other hand, will derive its powers from the States, as political and coequal societies; and these will be represented on the principle of equality in the Senate, as they now are in the existing Congress.

Our Founders were very careful to banish classes from the Constitution.

Could you imagine talking like this today? Basically, Mr. Madison is stating the importance of all peoples and states being equally represented in Congress. He is also proposing an idea for the Senate to represent the states, no particular class of people.

JAMES MADISON

ARTICLE I
Section 3

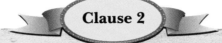

Clause 2

Immediately after they shall be assembled in Consequence of the first Election, they shall be divided as equally as may be into three Classes. The Seats of the Senators of the first Class shall be vacated at the Expiration of the second Year, of the second Class at the Expiration of the fourth Year, and of the third Class at the Expiration of the sixth Year, so that one third may be chosen every second Year; and if Vacancies happen by Resignation, or otherwise, during the Recess of the Legislature of any State, the Executive thereof may make temporary Appointments until the next Meeting of the Legislature, which shall then fill such Vacancies.

The Bottom Line

Article I, Section 3, Clause 2 outlines the election process for senators: Senators are elected every six years, but a third of the total senators are up for election every two years.

What Were They Thinking?

Our Founding Fathers wanted to make sure our government would be stable in order to prevent the instability that occurred under the Articles of Confederation. This resulted in our senatorial system of staggered elections.

Why Should I Care?

If it were not for this clause, every representative in the legislative branch would be up for reelection at once. Not only would that be a major campaign overload for us, but the legislative branch would be completely unpredictable, legislation would never be consistent, and congressional

ARTICLE Action

Under the Articles of Confederation, delegates were up for election all at once, so there was a possibility for significant turnover, which could lead to major instability in the government.

policies would change drastically every election cycle. Talk about bad policy.

Breakin' It Down

Our senatorial elections are different from any other election in our government. Our Founding Fathers split the Senate into three sections. (Envision cutting a pie into thirds.) The first third of the senators would be up for election in two years, a third in four years, and the last third of the senators would be up for election in six years. (Think of it as our Founding Fathers eating a pie, they are going to eat the first third of their pie in two days, the second third in four days, and the last third in six days.) When setting up the first senate in 1789, the Founders started this "thirds" process. In present day, each senator has a six-year term, but their elections are in staggered years.

Instability: Erratic, unpredictable. 2. Not steady: a lack of steadiness or firmness

Federalist Papers: A series of eighty-five essays written by Alexander Hamilton, James Madison, and John Jay in the late 1780s to persuade the voters of New York to adopt the Constitution. The essays are considered a classic defense of the American system of government, as well as a classic practical application of political principles.

How Can I Make a Difference?

See if your friends or family members know the election cycle for our Senate. Find out what cycle your Senators are in. Will they be up for election in two, four, or six years?

What Has It Done For Me Lately?

In 2010, the election fell in the favor of the Republicans. Even though the House changed majority, the Senate did not. Because of staggered elections, it was harder for the Republicans to take back the Senate.

> Our Founders put a lot of thought into stability of government.

★★

Founding Father Forum

James Madison came up with four reasons why constantly changing laws and instability are bad for government and wrote them down in Federalist Paper 62.

1. Foreign policy: The senate plays a huge role in foreign policy. If a new group of senators came in every six years, they might totally disagree with the previous senators and change where America stood on foreign policy. This would make us look to other countries like we couldn't be trusted in important, long-lasting matters. We would be changing our minds all the time!

2. Legislating laws: If laws were constantly changing, no person would ever know what the laws would be, and we would live in fear that the law would be one thing before the election and something totally different after the election!

3. Entrepreneurship: You wouldn't want to start your own business if you knew that the laws would change after every election cycle. Taxes would differ with each new set of congressmen!

4. Trust: Worst of all, the people would begin to distrust their legislators due to the lack of stability. We would begin to lose faith in our legislature and government as a whole.

ARTICLE I
Section 3

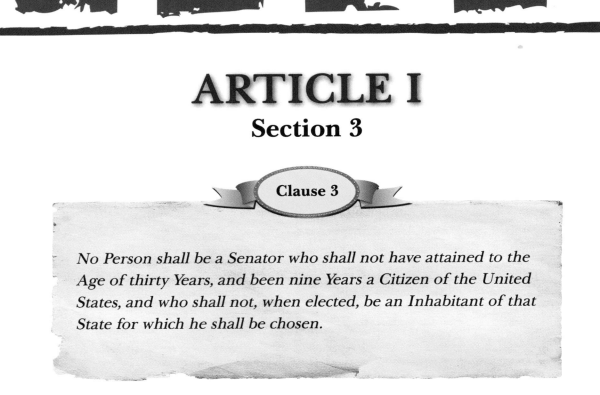

Clause 3

No Person shall be a Senator who shall not have attained to the Age of thirty Years, and been nine Years a Citizen of the United States, and who shall not, when elected, be an Inhabitant of that State for which he shall be chosen.

The Bottom Line

Article I, Section 3, Clause 3 sums up the requirements for being a senator.

What Were They Thinking?

At the time, our Founding Fathers felt being a senator carried more responsibility, so they wanted more "stability of character." They felt that a thirty-year-old person was more mature than a twenty-five-year old. Another reason is that our Founders felt being a senator carried more responsibility, so they wanted to give a person the option of first becoming a representative in the House before working their way up the ladder to becoming a senator.

Why Should I Care?

It's important to know the requirements for becoming a senator so you can judge a candidate's political maturity and experience when you are

Convention Chat

Our Founding Fathers wanted senators to live in the state he (or she) represented, so as "states men," they would have their state's best interest at heart.

voting, because there are instances of people trying to bend the Constitutional requirements, by writing someone onto the ballot, for example.

Breakin' It Down

Notice this clause closely resembles Article I, Section 2, Clauses 1-2 regarding the House Representative requirements, except senatorial requirements are slightly different. First, our Founders felt that a thirty-year-old person was more mature and better qualified for the gravitas of the Senate. Another idea behind this age difference was to allow candidates to first hold an office in the House before working their way up the ladder to becoming a senator.

Also notice the required citizenship is nine years versus seven to be a representative. This goes back to the newness of our nation at the time the Constitution was being drafted. Since the Senate deals with foreign policy, the Founders wanted their loyalties to lie with America and not some other "mother country." Last, a senator must be an inhabitant of the state which he is representing, but there are no requirements on living in your county or district.

How Can I Make a Difference?

Research senators who weren't born in America and where they immigrated from at www.senate.gov.

What Has It Done For Me Lately?

This clause remains a written checklist for our current senatorial candidates.

OUR BRITISH ROOTS

The idea of the Senate was borrowed from Britain's parliament. The Senate was meant to be more focused and "deliberative" than the House of Representatives—a body of "thinkers."

So Parliament is like our Congress but with a House of Lords and a House of Commons instead of senators and representatives.

LIBERTY Language

Gravitas: Seriousness or sobriety, as of conduct or speech.

Parliament: 1. A representative body having supreme legislative powers within a state or multinational organization. 2. The national legislature of the United Kingdom, made up of the House of Lords and the House of Commons.

ARTICLE I
Section 3

Clauses 4–5

⁴ *The Vice President of the United States shall be President of the Senate, but shall have no Vote, unless they be equally divided.*

⁵ *The Senate shall chuse their other Officers, and also a President pro tempore, in the Absence of the Vice President, or when he shall exercise the Office of President of the United States.*

The Bottom Line

Article I, Section 3, Clause 4 describes the role of our vice president: to preside over the Senate and to cast a vote only if there is a tied result during a vote on legislation. Article I, Section 3, Clause 5 states that the Senate is responsible for choosing a person to preside over the Senate in place of the Vice President when he is unable to do so.

What Were They Thinking?

Our Founding Fathers knew someone had to be the tie-breaker, so they gave the job to the vice president. They also knew the vice president would not always be available to preside over the Senate. So they gave the Senate the ability to appoint other officers when the vice president was away, kind of like a substitute teacher.

FOUNDING Father Forum

John Adams
★ Our nation's first vice president, from 1789-1797.
★ Our nation's second president, from 1797-1801.

Why Should I Care?

It's important that the vice president will always cast a tie-breaking vote. If this rule hadn't been established, the already lengthy process of creating legislation would take even longer (something we definitely don't need), or a biased person could be chosen to cast the tie-breaking vote, which would be totally unfair!

Breakin' It Down

This is the first time our Founding Fathers mention the role of vice president in the Constitution. Our nation's first vice president, John Adams, once described the role of VP as very insignificant and very boring. But really our Founding Fathers gave the VP very important jobs of presiding over the Senate and casting all tie-breaking votes. Clause 5 also shows our Founding Fathers' foresight when they gave the Senate the ability to elect a senator to be the temporary leader of the Senate when the vice president is not present in order to keep the Senate running.

BTW: Later the vice president was given two more key roles: to determine if a president becomes unable to perform, and replace the president if needed. Also, today the vice president works closely with the president and the executive branch.

FOUNDING Father Forum

★ John Adams called his job boring, because back then the VP had to sit in during sessions but had no vote on normal bills and laws—in other words, no say on any issues—unless there was a tie. But John Adams (Pop Quiz! **Our first VP**), cast his tie-breaking vote twenty-nine times.

> The role of vice president is the most insignificant office that ever the invention of man contrived or his imagination conceived.
>
> – In a letter to his wife Abigail

How Can I Make a Difference?

Find out how many times the vice president has cast the tie-breaking vote at www.senate.gov. Go to the mall and survey people to see if they know who casts the tie-breaker vote.

What Has It Done For Me Lately?

The VP still has the tie-breaking vote. Richard Cheney, the VP under President George W. Bush, cast his tie-breaking vote eight times!

LIBERTY Language

Pro tempore: Latin for temporary. President "pro tempore" would be a person who would temporarily preside over the Senate in place of the VP.

JOHN ADAMS

ARTICLE I
Section 3

6 The Senate shall have the sole Power to try all Impeachments. When sitting for that Purpose, they shall be on Oath or Affirmation. When the President of the United States is tried, the Chief Justice shall preside: And no Person shall be convicted without the Concurrence of two thirds of the Members present.

7 Judgment in Cases of impeachment shall not extend further than to removal from Office, and disqualification to hold and enjoy any Office of honor, Trust or Profit under the United States: but the Party convicted shall nevertheless be liable and subject to Indictment, Trial, Judgment and Punishment, according to Law.

Would it be possible to restate these clauses in easy-to-understand English?

The Bottom Line

Article I, Section 3, Clauses 6-7 outline the three-step process of impeachment:

1. After members of the House call for impeachment the trial takes place on the Senate floor.
2. The Chief Justice of the U.S. Supreme Court presides over the trial (if the president is being impeached).
3. Impeachment occurs if two-thirds of all present senate members agree.

What Were They Thinking?

Our Founding Fathers considered the impeachment process extremely important because it holds our politicians accountable and preserves the honesty and integrity of our government. They also wanted to ensure that all branches of government played a part, and this clause is another example of our excellent system of checks and balances.

Why Should I Care?

If the president (or any other officials in D.C.) engages in criminal conduct, you wouldn't be able to fire him or her without this clause—at least until the next election.

Breakin' It Down

Our Founding Fathers gave the Senate the authority to "try all impeachments," meaning that the impeached individual's trial would take place on the Senate floor.

Clause 6 also states that the chief justice of the U.S. Supreme Court will preside over the trial if the president is the individual being impeached, and no officer will be convicted without the agreement of two-thirds of all Senate members present. Whether or not an officer is impeached, he or she can still be tried in a court of law.

How Can I Make a Difference?

Follow the news to see whether any officials in the federal government are engaged in, or were ever engaged in, bribery or criminal conduct.

LIBERTY Language

Preside: Oversee, supervise, manage.

Pop Quiz! What's the most recent bit of legislation the president signed into law?

'Liar' is just as ugly a word as 'thief,' because it implies the presence of just as ugly a sin in one case as in the other. If a man lies under oath, or procures the lie of another under oath, if he perjures himself or suborns perjury, he is guilty under the statute law.

—THEODORE ROOSEVELT

wikimedia.com, public domain

The prosecution [of impeachments], will seldom fail to agitate the passions of the whole community, and to divide it into parties more or less friendly or inimical to the accused. The subjects of its jurisdiction are those offenses which proceed from the misconduct of public men, or, in other words, from the abuse or violation of some public trust, and they relate chiefly to injuries done immediately to the society itself.

ALEXANDER HAMILTON

What Hamilton is saying here is that when a president is impeached, his trial gets people riled up because when a president (or a "public man") does something wrong, the people feel like he's violated and abused their trust.

What Has It Done For Me Lately?

When you think of impeachment, you might automatically think of the president, but any government official can be impeached. In late 2010, federal judge G. Thomas Porteous was convicted of lying to the FBI, making him the eighth federal judge in the nation's history to be impeached.

All in all, the Framers would probably agree that it's better to impeach too often than too seldom. If presidents can't be virtuous, they should at least be nervous.
– Joseph Sobran

Pop Quiz! We learned the House has the power to call for impeachment, but they don't have the authority to impeach ALONE.

ARTICLE I
Section 4

Clauses 1–2

¹The Times, Places and Manner of holding Elections for Senators and Representatives, shall be prescribed in each State by the Legislature thereof; but the Congress may at any time by Law make or alter such Regulations, except as to the Places of chusing Senators.

²The Congress shall assemble at least once in every Year, and such Meeting shall be on the first Monday in December, unless they shall by Law appoint a different Day.

The Bottom Line

Article I, Section 4, Clauses 1–2 required each state to hold predictable and standardized elections so that the states will always send a representative to Congress. Congress must also meet at least once a year.

What Were They Thinking?

Under the Articles of Confederation, there were times when a certain state, for whatever reason, did not hold elections or send representatives to Congress. The government couldn't run without the legislative branch. So in the Constitution, the Framers ordered each state to hold national elections.

Why Should I Care?

If Congress doesn't show up, then there is no representation for the people. Talk about taxation without representation!

Breakin' It Down

These clauses give the states the responsibility to choose the place, time, and management of legislative elections, however, congress could alter these regulations. Meaning, if the states didn't follow through, the federal congress would do it for them. This actually occurred in 1842, because the states were not adhering to their duties and sending representatives to Washington, D.C.

Today, all federal, general elections are held on the same day and at the same time. States still have the sole power of recounting the votes in a very close election. (We all know how important that is!) And each state has its own rules on replacing candidates who drop out of the races unexpectedly right before the election.

This clause also mandates Congress meets every year.

ARTICLE Action

If our Founding Fathers hadn't established this clause, the president could control when and how often Congress meets during their terms in office. Before the Revolutionary War, the colonial governors—under control of the British King—determined when and how often Congress met.

How Can I Make a Difference?

Write out five or more questions on what you have learned about Congress so far. Survey your neighbors and find out how many people can answer all five questions correctly.

What Has It Done For Me Lately?

Thanks to this clause in the Constitution, the senators and representatives we elect into office are ordered to meet at least once a year during their term. Today, however, our representatives in Washington, D.C. meet pretty much all year, except for a few recesses.

Every government ought to contain in itself the means of its own preservation.

ALEXANDER HAMILTON

ARTICLE I
Section 5

Clause 1

Each House shall be the Judge of the Elections, Returns and Qualifications of its own Members, and a Majority of each shall constitute a Quorum to do Business; but a smaller Number may adjourn from day to day, and may be authorized to compel the Attendance of absent Members, in such Manner, and under such Penalties as each House may provide.

The Bottom Line

Article I, Section 5, Clause 1 says Congress is responsible for making sure the new representatives meet all the constitutional qualifications, and that a majority of representatives have to be present in order to do business.

What Were They Thinking?

Our Founding Fathers wanted to make sure there weren't any unqualified people in Congress, and the laws of the country weren't being passed by only four representatives. So they established that a quorum, or majority, has to be present to do business. Smart call.

Why Should I Care?

If the majority of our representatives were not present during congressional assembly, who knows what kinds of bills could be passed? If our Founding Fathers hadn't set the quorum in place, two representatives could gather on some holiday and pass a bill saying that all cell phones must be turned off at 9:00 at night! I doubt that bill would go very far, but you never know.

LIBERTY Language

Quorum: The number of people that have to be present in order for the legislature to do business.

> It would be a pleasing ground of confidence to the people that no law or burden could be imposed on them, by a few men.

Breakin' It Down

Clause 1 gives our legislature the ability to determine whether or not a new representative fits the bill, so to speak, in regard to constitutional requirements.

The "Quorum" part of the clause means a majority of members must be present to vote. In the modern-day U.S. Senate, there are one hundred senators, and the quorum is set at fifty-one percent, or fifty-one members. That's the majority, but just barely! This is called a simple majority. The forty-nine other senators are allowed to adjourn, or leave, for a few days, but the majority is authorized to call them back when needed.

> What would our Founding Fathers think of this?

How Can I Make a Difference?

Check the Congress voting record and see if your representative has been present for the votes. How regularly did he or she vote?

What Has It Done For Me Lately?

The Democratic Leaders of the Wisconsin state legislature left the state in order to prove a political point, leaving too few members in Wisconsin to meet quorum standards. Meaning, there was not a majority present. The Wisconsin legislature was at a standstill until the members returned. This could happen in our national legislature!

OLIVER ELLSWORTH

ARTICLE I
Section 5

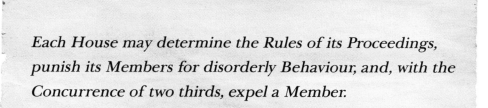

Clause 2

Each House may determine the Rules of its Proceedings, punish its Members for disorderly Behaviour, and, with the Concurrence of two thirds, expel a Member.

The Bottom Line
Article I, Section 5, Clause 2 says the Senate and the House can establish their own rules and guidelines for proceedings, and they can kick someone out for bad behavior—as long as two-thirds agrees.

What Were They Thinking?
Our Founding Fathers wanted to make sure that each new Congress could change and improve its rules and guidelines and also be able to fire members for bad behavior.

Why Should I Care?
Let's say that your state sends a representative to Congress, but your representative plays Wii Fitness all day, every day, and never shows up to vote. Now, instead of having to go through a whole congressional term without representation, the Congress can vote

to expel this representative, and if two-thirds of the representatives agree, then this representative will be sent back home where he or she will be free to play Wii uninterrupted. And then a special election will be scheduled to replace that person, like we learned from Article I, Section 2, Clause 4. Actually, this clause comes to play if a representative has continual disorderly behavior, such as drunkenness or immorality, and this clause would hold your representatives accountable for his actions.

Breakin' It Down

Each house writes its own rules, which can be revised after each election. The two branches are very different from each other, and it simply wouldn't work for the Senate to create the House's rules for procedures and vice-versa.

And if a legislature wasn't able to update its rules, then our Congress today would still be under the same procedural rules of our very first Congress. Think about it!

Similarly, firing a member for bad behavior may seem like common sense, but stating it in the Constitution provides a check on the behaviors of congressional members.

Filibuster: Right or Tactic?

To delay or block a vote on a bill, senators can filibuster. A filibuster is a delay tactic where a senator talks so long the Senate can't vote on a bill. It's not available in the House, and the record is held by Senator Strom Thurmond, who filibustered the Civil Rights Act of 1957 by talking continuously for more than 24 hours. Since 1917, a filibuster could be ended by passing a cloture (French for "closure") motion, though this is rarely used because it needs three-fifths of the Senate members present to pass.

How Can I Make a Difference?

Search www.rules.house.gov and www.rules.senate.gov to find the rules established by the current Congress. How do the rules compare to previous rules? Do you agree or disagree?

What Has It Done For Me Lately?

In January 2011, the House of Representatives added to their proceedings a rule saying every law must have constitutional justification before it can be considered for a vote. They also held a meeting at the beginning of the 112th Congress to read aloud the entire Constitution.

ARTICLE I
Section 5

Clauses 3–4

³Each House shall keep a Journal of its Proceedings, and from time to time publish the same, excepting such Parts as may in their Judgment require Secrecy; and the Yeas and Nays of the Members of either House on any question shall, at the Desire of one fifth of those Present, be entered on the Journal.

⁴Neither House, during the Session of Congress, shall, without the Consent of the other, adjourn for more than three days, nor to any other Place than that in which the two Houses shall be sitting.

The Bottom Line
Article I, Section 5, Clauses 3–4 requires the House and Senate to keep a public record of their meetings, and said neither house can adjourn without permission of the other house, and they must meet in the same location.

What Were They Thinking?
Our Founding Fathers wanted to make sure Congress didn't hide its proceedings from the public.

Why Should I Care?
Thanks to this clause, we can always know what's going on in our Congress. Otherwise, Congress could choose what to tell and what to hide from the public. Congressional proceedings must be open to the public. Congress cannot legislate in secrecy.

Breakin' It Down
So we learned Congress must keep a public record of their business, but why can't one branch adjourn without consent from the other?

BTW: The transcripts of the legislature's proceedings were first begun by private businesses. From 1789–1873, there were three different transcripts of the legislature's business. The 36th Congress, ending in 1861, decided the transcripts should be reprinted as the Congressional Record and federally funded, and so began the Congressional Record that we use today.

Because, during breaks from activity, the president could feasibly perform some action, like appointing a new officer or vetoing a bill with just the House present. It is unconstitutional for the president to do both of these actions without giving the legislative branch an opportunity to respond. For one branch to adjourn prematurely will prevent the other branch from doing the people's business.

How Can I Make a Difference?

Read the record of a congressional proceeding that took place during the time of our Founding Fathers, and compare it with a record from today. Note the differences. See any similarities?

What Has It Done For Me Lately?

Along with the congressional record, CSPAN is our "written" record of congressional proceedings. CSPAN is a privately owned transcript business. It began filming the House in 1979 and the Senate in 1986. This is one example of how the media has helped keep Congress open to the public.

Who says our government hasn't caught up with the times?

Convention Chat

Our Founding Fathers looked to other examples of civilizations and governments that recorded their proceedings. From the Sumerians in 2500 B.C., to the Egyptians, to the British parliament, civilizations have been recording their works since the beginning of time! So it's no surprise our Founding Fathers made this a requirement in both the Articles of Confederation and the Constitution.

COLONIAL Compare and Contrast

Adjourn v. Recess

Adjourn: An adjournment is a formal end to the business that was taking place on the chamber floor. When they return, they will not resume where they left off, they will pick up on a new subject. But if one member asks to return to the previous subject, they must, without filibuster or delay, return to the last subject.

Recess: A recess is a temporary halt from activity or debate on the floor. When they all return, they will pick up where they left off.

Both can last from twelve minutes to a number of weeks.

BTW: After the government took charge of transcribing what was said, a little editing began to take place. Members of the legislature, after the debate had already taken place, would add what they "meant to say" or "clarify" what they had said. With today's "instant media," like television and the Internet, our congressmen and women no longer have the advantage of "clarifying" before going to print. Now they get to clarify after they are called out by the media.

ARTICLE I
Section 6

Clause 1

The Senators and Representatives shall receive a Compensation for their Services, to be ascertained by Law, and paid out of the Treasury of the United States. They shall in all Cases, except Treason, Felony and Breach of the Peace, be privileged from Arrest during their Attendance at the Session of their respective Houses, and in going to and returning from the same; and for any Speech or Debate in either House, they shall not be questioned in any other Place.

The Bottom Line

Article I, Section 6, Clause 1 makes sure representatives get paid. The second part is known as the "Speech or Debate Clause," and it protects members of Congress from being arrested for things said during proceedings.

What Were They Thinking?

Our Founding Fathers wanted representatives paid for their work, and they trusted the people to provide a check on Congress if their salaries were too high. Our Founding Fathers also wanted to make sure no senator or representative would be punished for an argument or debate they had while in session.

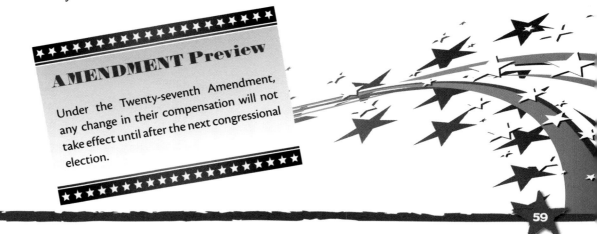

AMENDMENT Preview

Under the Twenty-seventh Amendment, any change in their compensation will not take effect until after the next congressional election.

Why Should I Care?

This clause in the Constitution protects our representatives' safety and freedom of speech. Thanks to this clause, our representatives can fully voice their opinion without fear of arrest.

Breakin' It Down

Our Founders felt all representatives should be paid by the National Treasury, and the amount was left to Congress, with the understanding that voters are watching.

The second part of this clause is known as the "Speech or Debate Clause." This clause in the Constitution protects our representatives from being imprisoned for something said in Congress, or falsely accused of some crime or sent to jail for speaking against their president or any other branch of government—which actually happened in British Parliament! (The king could arrest a member for saying things he didn't like.) This would be a violation of our freedom of speech and prevent some representatives from being up front on controversial issues that need to be addressed!

How Can I Make a Difference?

Many representatives take for granted that they can speak freely in Congress. Send your representative an email or letter about an issue important to you, or just to say thanks for all the hard work.

What Has It Done For Me Lately?

Today, in many other countries around the world, people (including government officials) are thrown in jail for speaking against authority. In America, just as the Constitution protects our freedom of speech, it protects the speech of our representatives in Congress, which is vital for liberty.

OUR BRITISH ROOTS

The "Speech and Debate" issue was mentioned in the English Bill of Rights of 1689.

ARTICLE Action

Under the Articles of Confederation, every representative was paid by the state he represented. However, Rhode Island (or "Rogue Island" as President George Washington called the state) had failed to pay their representative, and so was not represented in the Confederation Congress. During the Constitutional Convention, this issue arose again. Our Founders agreed that the representatives should be paid, not from the states they represented, but from the National Treasury, or the federal government's bank.

ARTICLE I
Section 6

Clause 2

No Senator or Representative shall, during the Time for which he was elected, be appointed to any civil Office under the Authority of the United States, which shall have been created, or the Emoluments whereof shall have been encreased during such time; and no Person holding any Office under the United States, shall be a Member of either House during his Continuance in Office.

The Bottom Line
Article I, Section 6, Clause 2 has two different names: the "Emoluments Clause," which prevents congressmen from being appointed to a position in which he voted to increase the salary; and the "Incompatibility Clause," which prevents congressmen from holding two offices at once.

What Were They Thinking?
Our Founding Fathers wanted to make sure that the president would not be able to create new cabinet positions for sitting members of Congress, which would spark bribery and corruption between the two branches. Also, they wanted to prevent a congressman or woman from voting to raise the salary of a position and then be appointed to the same position.

Why Should I Care?
This clause prevents bribery and corruption from occurring within Congress and between the other branches of government. It makes sure that the people are represented by honest people.

Debate

Read the actual words spoken by our Framers.

In America, legislative bodies have reduced their own wages lower, rather than augmented them. This is a power which cannot be abused without rousing universal attention and indignation. What would be the consequence of the Virginian legislature raising their pay to four or five pounds each per day? The universal indignation of the people.

The pay of the members is, by the Constitution, to be fixed by themselves, without limitation or restraint. They may therefore indulge themselves in the fullest extent. They may make their compensation as high as they please.

He's saying the people would prevent congressmen from raising their salaries too high.

MR. HENRY

JAMES MADISON

If their pay wasn't fair, and not enough to live on, then only the rich would be able to afford to hold an office because they would have outside income. And that would result in a Congress full of rich folk—definitely not an equal representation of the people.

The observations made by several honorable members illustrate my opinion, that it is impossible to devise any system agreeable to all. When objections so contradictory are brought against it, how shall we decide? Some gentlemen object to it because they may make their wages too high; others object to it because they may make them too low. If it is to be perpetually attacked by principles so repugnant, we may cease to discuss. For what is the object of our discussion? Truth, sir. To draw a true and just conclusion.

I felt that, as their compensations were not fixed in the Constitution, Congress might fix them so low, that none but rich men could go; by which the government might terminate in an aristocracy.

It's impossible to come up with a solution to please everyone, and in certain areas, they had to rely on faith and trust in the American people and the government created by the Constitution—a government founded on Christian principles.

MR. TYLER

JAMES MADISON

It is impossible to rightly govern a nation without God and the Bible.

GEORGE WASHINGTON

Breakin' It Down

The first half of this clause is known as the "Emoluments Clause," and the second half is known as the "Incompatibility Clause."

James Madison saw this clause as a very important check on potential illegal or secret cabinet appointments by the president. Madison, along with our other Founding Fathers, wanted to prevent the president from creating cabinet positions for sitting members of Congress. Madison also wanted to prevent a representative from voting to raise the pay of a position he or she was about to be appointed to.

This has happened many times in our country's history. For example, in 1909, President Taft nominated Senator Philander Knox to be Secretary of State. Knox had just voted to increase the salary of that position by $4,000! Congress then lowered the salary from $12,000 to the original $8,000 and Knox took the position.

The second half of this clause, the "Incompatibility Clause," makes sure that a representative does not hold two political positions at once. President George Washington wanted to appoint Senator William Patterson to the Supreme Court, but Patterson was still in the middle of his senatorial term. So President Washington waited until Patterson's term expired before appointing him to the Supreme Court.

How Can I Make a Difference?

Research www.senate.gov and find out the last time Congress raised their salary. Do you agree with the amount they are receiving?

What Has It Done For Me Lately?

While Senator Hilary Clinton and Senator Ken Salazar were still in the Senate, the pay for cabinet officers was increased. So when they were appointed Secretary of State and Secretary of the Interior, their pay had to be reduced to the former level of those offices.

ARTICLE I
Section 7

Clause 1

All Bills for raising Revenue shall originate in the House of Representatives; but the Senate may propose or concur with Amendments as on other Bills.

The Bottom Line

Article I, Section 7, Clause 1 establishes all laws or bills regarding money would be created by the House of Representatives, but the Senate could amend these bills.

What Were They Thinking?

We know that the House of Representatives is the house closest to the people, right? Because of this, our Founders thought it fitting for the House to be in charge of the money, so the people would be heard and their needs provided for — the people would really be the ones proposing the legislation.

> Our Founding Fathers wanted the balance of power to come into play in every way possible.

Why Should I Care?

The money spent by Congress comes from our parents' paychecks (and some-day our paychecks, too). Any money spent by Congress comes mostly from We the People.

Breakin' It Down

All bills relating to raising money for the national government are to originate in the House of Representatives. The senators have the ability to adjust the bill by adding an amendment.

Sadly, today this clause is misused. Instead of the Senate adding an amendment to the bill, they alter the bill so much that sometimes the intention of the original bill is completely distorted. Sometimes the Senate erases everything in the original bill except "Be It Hereby Enacted" (the first four words in every bill).

Looking over an actual piece of legislation kind of shows why our officials deserve to be paid for what they're doing.

How Can I Make a Difference?

Want to see what I mean? Look up a piece of legislation at www.thomas.gov. Go a step further and look up a piece of legislation that addressed an issue on money. Compare the original legislation that passed through the House with the final legislation that went through the Senate. Notice any revisions? Do you agree?

What Has It Done For Me Lately?

Legislation regarding money is proposed constantly by the House of Representatives, but few reach the president's desk because the Senate only passes the monetary legislation they see fitting for the country.

Taxes imposed on the colonists by the Parliament weren't fair because they didn't have anyone in Parliament to stand up for their colonial rights or represent their needs.

BTW: English taxes were called "gifts from the commons to the crown." They were not forced onto the people, rather, the commoners were supposed to "give" money to their government.

ARTICLE I
Section 7

Clause 2

Every Bill which shall have passed the House of Representatives and the Senate, shall, before it become a Law, be presented to the President of the United States; if he approve he shall sign it, but if not he shall return it, with his Objections to that House in which it shall have originated, who shall enter the Objections at large on their Journal, and proceed to reconsider it. If after such Reconsideration two thirds of that House shall agree to pass the Bill, it shall be sent, together with the Objections, to the other House, by which it shall likewise be reconsidered, and if approved by two thirds of that House, it shall become a Law. But in all such Cases the Votes of both Houses shall be determined by Yeas and Nays, and the Names of the Persons voting for and against the Bill shall be entered on the Journal of each House respectively. If any Bill shall not be returned by the President within ten Days (Sundays excepted) after it shall have been presented to him, the Same shall be a Law, in like Manner as if he had signed it, unless the Congress by their Adjournment prevent its Return, in which Case it shall not be a Law.

The Bottom Line
Article I, Section 7, Clause 2 establishes the presidential veto power.

What Were They Thinking?
The president's veto power is another example of our Founders' system of checks and balances. Congress is the only branch that can enact new legislation, but the legislation must be approved by the president before it can become law.

Why Should I Care?

Without a check on the legislative branch, Congress could pass any random bill into law, such as a ban against all cell phone use outside your home. Fortunately, the president has veto power to prevent the bill from becoming law. Veto power could save the public use of cell phones!

Breakin' It Down

Each branch of our government holds very specific jobs regarding laws. Congress is granted the sole ability to legislate, the president has the sole authority to execute the laws, and the courts have the sole power to judge according to those laws.

Through veto power, our Founders established a happy medium between not enough and too much separation of power. The Congress is in control of creating legislation, but the president has the power to approve or disapprove. The president has the power to prevent a bill from becoming a law that he feels is detrimental, but he can't enact new laws. This is a balance of power.

How Can I Make a Difference?

Find out how many times the president has vetoed a bill in the past twenty years at http://artandhistory.house.gov. Look into two or more of the vetoed bills. Do you agree with the president's actions?

What Has It Done For Me Lately?

President Obama has used his veto power twice. President George W. Bush before him used the power of the veto twelve times. President Clinton used the veto thirty-seven times! FDR used his veto power 635 times!

FOUNDING Father Forum

★ Alexander Hamilton argued that the president should have absolute veto. Instead, it was agreed a president's veto could be overruled — if two-thirds of Congress approves.

The veto must exist and be used to prevent unjust and pernicious laws.

It is necessary to make the president the guardian of the people, even of the lower classes, against legislative tyranny, against the great and the wealthy who in the course of things will necessarily compose the legislative body.

Checks and balances are found throughout the entire Constitution and show the great forethought our Founders put into creating our United States.

GEORGE MASON

GOUVERNEUR MORRIS

ARTICLE I
Section 7

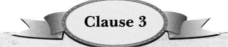

Clause 3

Every Order, Resolution, or Vote to which the Concurrence of the Senate and House of Representatives may be necessary (except on a question of Adjournment) shall be presented to the President of the United States; and before the Same shall take Effect, shall be approved by him, or being disapproved by him, shall be repassed by two thirds of the Senate and House of Representatives, according to the Rules and Limitations prescribed in the Case of a Bill.

The Bottom Line

Article I, Section 7, Clause 3 says if the president does veto a bill, it can be reevaluated by the Congress and made into law if both the House and the Senate pass it with a two-thirds majority.

What Were They Thinking?

Fear of executive power was widespread during colonial America. Our Founders didn't trust giving the executive branch complete authority.

Why Should I Care?

Let's say Congress passed a law that police couldn't arrest someone for video-taping on their phone in public, but the president vetoes it. If two-thirds majority in both the House and Senate go back and vote in favor of the bill, that bill can become law. It prevents the president from overpowering the will of the people.

Breakin' It Down

A bill or law must first be voted on and passed by the House, or the people's chamber. Then the bill would go to the Senate for a vote. If the bill passes in both houses, the bill goes to the president's desk, and there it awaits his approval. If he finds that the bill or law runs against the country's best interest, he vetoes it. But if a law is important enough, if the people disagree strongly enough, the bill may come back to Congress, and if two-thirds majority vote in favor of the bill in both houses, the bill is passed into law.

How Can I Make a Difference?

Watch CSPAN and follow a bill as it passes from House to Senate. See if the president executes or vetos it.

What Has It Done For Me Lately?

Four vetoes were overridden by Congress under President George W. Bush. Before him, two vetoes were overridden by Congress under President Bill Clinton.

Not so fast, Mr. President! But the bill would have to be pretty important for it to pass Congress after a veto. Getting two-thirds majority in both houses to agree is no small feat!

ARTICLE I
Section 8

Clause 1

The Congress shall have Power To lay and collect Taxes, Duties, Imposts and Excises, to pay the Debts and provide for the common Defence and general Welfare of the United States; but all Duties, Imposts and Excises shall be uniform throughout the United States;

The Bottom Line

Article I, Section 8 has a lot of clauses that outline the duties of Congress. Article I, Section 8, Clause 1 gives Congress power to levy and collect taxes in order to finance government operations, but all federal taxes must have the same rate nationwide.

What Were They Thinking?

Our Founding Fathers wanted to create a government of "enumerated" powers, so they had to give a detailed list of the abilities of that government. Article I, Section 8, Clause 1 begins the enumeration, or numbered listings, of the abilities and powers of the Congress.

Why Should I Care?

Having a Constitution with enumerated powers is important because Congress can only do what is written down and no more. If the

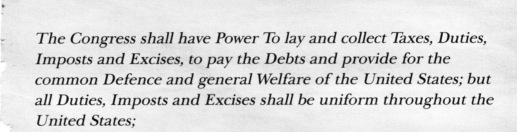

Constitution had instead listed what Congress *couldn't* do, then the power of our Congress would be much greater. For example, we can be pretty certain that our Founders wouldn't have mentioned Facebook in the Constitution, so if our Founding Fathers had only established what Congress couldn't do, then Congress could be free to regulate Facebook postings. That would be bad. This clause can actually be considered dangerous! Read on to find out why.

There is danger in this clause.

Breakin' It Down

The first way to view this clause is Congress only has the power to collect taxes to obtain federal funds. This federal money may be used to provide for the welfare of the people, for defense, paying debts, etc. This is the view that the Supreme Court follows.

The second view of this clause is that Congress can pass *any* kind of law, as long as it is for the welfare of all Americans. This interpretation would make Congress very powerful, and there would be no need for the limited powers of the Constitution. The Supreme Court has rejected this view.

There is danger in this clause. One view implies Congress can take money from taxpayers (federal income tax), and then give some of the money back to the states, but they can order the states to use the money however Congress says. This is essentially bribery. "We'll give you money, but only if you do what we say." For example, Congress can't force kids to study the history of the Constitution in school. However, Congress *can* offer money to the schools and fund school programs, but in return the school has to agree to teach a lesson on the Constitution. In this way Congress could control what is being taught in the schools. (This is just an example!)

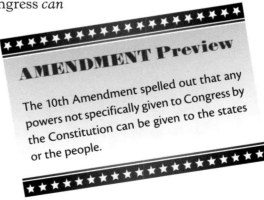

AMENDMENT Preview

The 10th Amendment spelled out that any powers not specifically given to Congress by the Constitution can be given to the states or the people.

BTW: Because the Constitution writes out specific powers for Congress, our government is considered one of LIMITS. If the Constitution was silent on specific powers, our government would basically have unlimited powers. Fortunately, our government only has the powers granted under the Constitution.

How Can I Make a Difference?

Check out www.thomas.gov and research a bill regarding taxes. Find out how it was executed through the U.S.

What Has It Done For Me Lately?

Medicaid or Medicare are extremely helpful to many Americans, but our Founding Fathers actually did not intend for the government to spend taxpayer money to take care of "favored" companies or individuals; rather, Alexander Hamilton thought "General Welfare" consisted of things like building roads that benefited all Americans.

Convention Chat

The meaning of "General Welfare" was hotly debated by James Madison and Alexander Hamilton. Madison believed Congress should only spend money on purposes listed in the Constitution. Hamilton argued Congress could spend money on anything that benefitted Americans as a whole.

> Pretty controversial, eh? If the people who wrote it had a hard time deciphering the meaning, we shouldn't feel too bad.

ARTICLE I
Section 8

Clause 2

To borrow Money on the credit of the United States;

The Bottom Line
Article I, Section 8, Clause 2 states that Congress has the ability to borrow the money on the credit of the U.S.

What Were They Thinking?
Our Founding Fathers had to borrow money from other countries during the Revolutionary War. As a result, they wanted Congress to have the ability to borrow money for America when needed. But they wanted the ability to be based on the credit of the U.S. so that other countries would respect America.

Why Should I Care?
When you go to the mall with your friends, you may ask to borrow your parents' credit card to buy food or something you spot in a window. However, your parents will only give you a credit card if they know you are responsible with it. This is very similar to how Congress can borrow money. Congress is allowed to ask other countries for loans, but the foreign

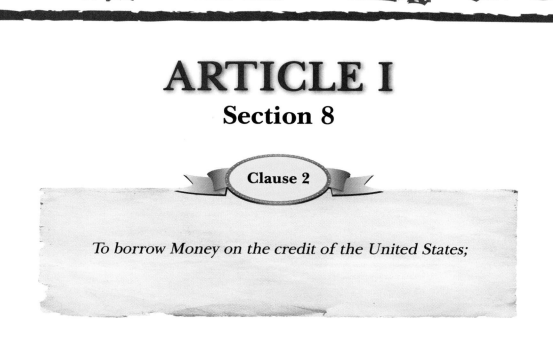

FOUNDING Father Forum

★ During the Revolutionary War, the colonies were in a fix. We had previously been under the rule of England, under English banks, and the British had disabled our banking system, so we did not have the money to fund the war. However, John Adams and a handful of other Founding Fathers traveled to the Netherlands and negotiated with the Dutch to grant us a loan.

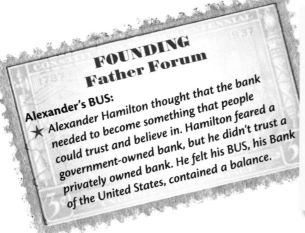

ARTICLE Action

Before the Constitutional Convention, Alexander Hamilton saw a need for a solid banking system, but under the Articles of Confederation, Congress wasn't allowed to grant charters to banks or other corporations. So Alexander Hamilton's first idea for the Bank of North America failed because he couldn't obtain a charter for the bank. But the pattern was set for his second bank, The Bank of the United States (or the BUS).

countries will only give us money because they know we are responsible with it.

Breakin' It Down

"To borrow Money on the Credit of the United States." This clause grants Congress the constitutional ability to borrow money based on the United States' credit.

How Can I Make a Difference?

Check out the U.S. Debt Clock at www.usdebtclock.org. Make a list of the countries we owe money.

What Has It Done For Me Lately?

This clause is used by our Congress more than they ever intended. We currently are 15 trillion dollars in debt! From January 2010 to January 2011, our federal government borrowed $1.8 trillion, or five billion dollars a day.

What's a charter, you may be wondering.

LIBERTY Language

Bank Charter: An official document authorizing the operation of a bank, including the articles of incorporation and the certificate of incorporation.

Credit: In this sense it means a record of your payment history. If you walk into a bank and ask to borrow money, they will look at your credit. If you always pay your bills two months late, you will have "bad credit," and most likely the bank will not give you the loan. In Congressional terms, if we ask France for two million dollars to fund a new road program (borrow the money), they will look at the U.S. credit, and then assess the loan.

ARTICLE I
Section 8

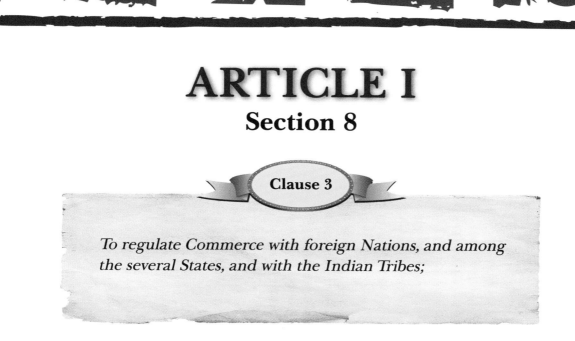

Clause 3

To regulate Commerce with foreign Nations, and among the several States, and with the Indian Tribes;

The Bottom Line

Article I, Section 8, Clause 3 is known as the "Commerce Clause," and gives Congress the ability to regulate trade with foreign nations and within the United States.

What Were They Thinking?

Our Founding Fathers wanted a single body to regulate trade to create consistency for trade between states and with other nations.

Why Should I Care?

Without regulation, trade prices could change drastically between states and foreign countries, or foreign countries might not want to trade with us, which would seriously impact the imports of everything from iPhones to stuffed animals to paper.

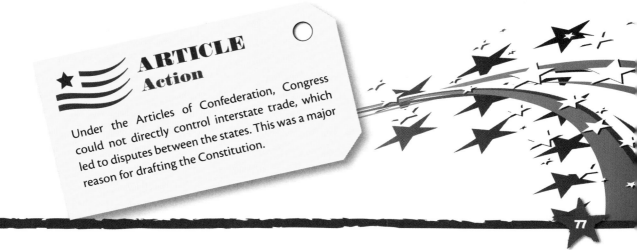

ARTICLE Action

Under the Articles of Confederation, Congress could not directly control interstate trade, which led to disputes between the states. This was a major reason for drafting the Constitution.

Breakin' It Down

This clause allows Congress to regulate commerce with other nations, such as maintaining prices and taxes on imports and exports and regulate commerce between the states (see box below).

(see box below)

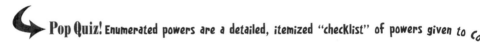

How Can I Make a Difference?

Research how much money we are taxed by China to import their goods into our country. Then compare that with how much we charge China to import our goods. Do you find this fair?

What Has It Done For Me Lately?

Congress still regulates all goods that come into the United States from other countries. Any product that comes from other countries to be sold in America is monitored by Congress until it is distributed to the customers.

Pop Quiz! Enumerated powers are a detailed, itemized "checklist" of powers given to Congress by our Founding Fathers and the Constitution.

★★

The Commerce Clause Goes to Court

Supreme Statements at the Supreme Court:

- The Supreme Court case *Gibbons v. Ogden* was called the "Steamboat case." A river barge had been granted a monopoly by New York State over a river crossing, so only a barge could transport goods and people over the river. Later, a steamboat company came along and wanted to cross at the same place. To the Supreme Court they went!

   Chief Justice John Marshall ruled that the monopoly granted the barge was unconstitutional, and that the federal government had the authority to address this issue because of the Commerce Clause — the river provided transportation of goods into New Jersey. A company could use this river to get its product into another state. Since the river was a way of transportation, one state could not prevent residents of another state from using the river.

- In another Supreme Court case, *Wickard v. Filburn*, the Supreme Court ruled that Congress could regulate how much wheat a farmer could grow. The wheat would be sold as a means of commerce, correct? Do you think the Court took the commerce clause too far in this ruling? How far did our Founding Fathers intend our federal government to take this clause?

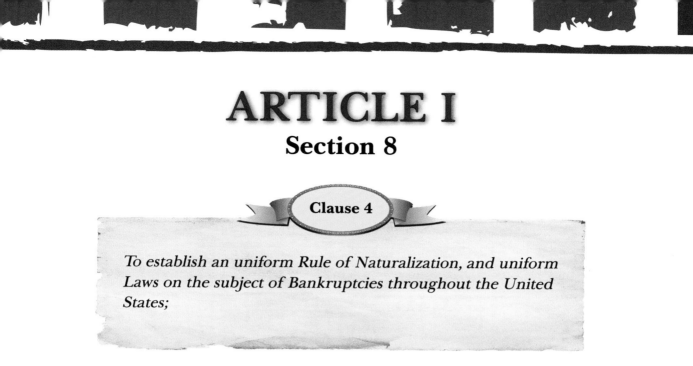

ARTICLE I
Section 8

Clause 4

To establish an uniform Rule of Naturalization, and uniform Laws on the subject of Bankruptcies throughout the United States;

The Bottom Line

Article I, Section 8, Clause 4 says Congress would establish the rules to become a citizen and create uniformity on the subject of bankruptcy.

What Were They Thinking?

Our Founding Fathers wanted Congress to be in charge of citizenship so that it would not become a state-wide issue. This would cause problems when traveling from one state to another, and it would also make people feel they were citizens of a certain state and not the United States of America as a whole. As for bankruptcy, our Founding Fathers also wanted to do away with the "debtor's prison."

ARTICLE Action

Under the Articles of Confederation, naturalization was left up to the states.

Why Should I Care?

We already have enough to deal with when we travel. What if we had to have a passport to travel from state to state? If Congress was not in charge of American citizenship, we would have to carry a passport with us on all of our family road trips, because each state would have different citizenship policies. We would end up being citizens of our state and not America.

Breakin' It Down

This clause gives Congress authority to establish national rules for naturalization and bankruptcy.

Naturalization is the process of becoming a citizen of the U.S. As far back as the Roman Empire, nations have distinguished between citizens and aliens (a visitor, foreigner, or temporary resident—not a little green man from Mars). Since our Founders immigrated from other countries, they considered this an important issue and decided to grant this power to Congress to create unity among the states and make traveling or moving easier. Only the federal government, not the states, can determine who becomes a citizen.

ARTICLE Action

Bankruptcy laws make provisions for individuals or corporations that fail to pay their debts. Under the Articles of Confederation, states were still throwing debtors in jail, like the British. Many influential figures were thrown in debtor's prison, such as Robert Morris. Today, since this power was granted to Congress, the debtor's prison was abolished, and citizens now have a right to initiate bankruptcy themselves instead of waiting for their creditors to do it. Debtors still have to pay their debts as best they can through debt restructuring.

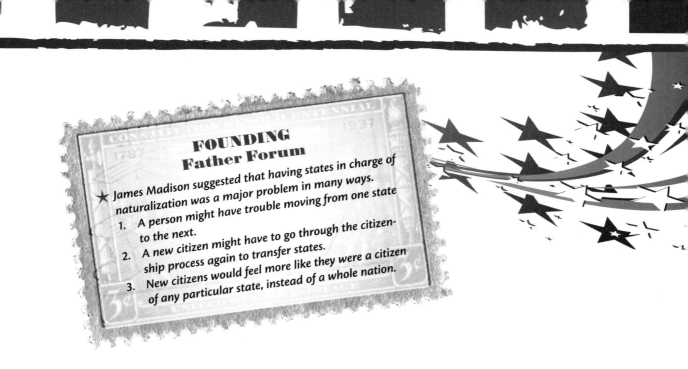

How Can I Make a Difference?

Talk to someone you know who has become a U.S. citizen, and see how much they know about the Constitution compared to you.

What Has It Done For Me Lately?

Today, illegal immigration is a large issue in politics. For one reason, illegal immigrants are willing to work for a fraction of minimum wage, which takes jobs away from American citizens. Illegal immigration is also an issue because foreignors crossing our border could endanger our national security. On the other hand, it also results in the illegal immigrants being exploited, or taken advantage of, by employers. According to this clause, it's up to Congress to establish legislation on how to handle this issue.

OUR BRITISH ROOTS

In 1542, under Henry VIII, a bankrupt person was considered a criminal and thrown into debtor's prison or hanged. However, in the early 1800s, the British adopted a new way of thinking and decided that a bankrupt person would not be punished, but would have to pay his debts as much as he could.

ARTICLE I
Section 8

⁵To coin Money, regulate the Value thereof, and of foreign Coin, and fix the Standard of Weights and Measures;

⁶To provide for the Punishment of counterfeiting the Securities and current Coin of the United States;

The Bottom Line

Article I, Section 8, Clauses 5–6 give Congress authority to coin and value money, determine value of foreign money, establish a system of weights and measures, and punish those guilty of counterfeiting.

What Were They Thinking?

Our Founding Fathers saw that the states had all accumulated masses of debt after the Revolutionary War and that each state was making different forms of currency. Inflation began to emerge as a hot topic, just as it is today. They also saw that there needed to be a uniformity regarding the value of foreign coins. So our Framers took the power of coining money from the states and placed it into the federal government's hands, as well as the ability to regulate the value of foreign coins.

Why Should I Care?

The American money system would be completely out of whack if it wasn't regulated by Congress. If each state was in charge of regulating its own money, then we would have to exchange our money when we wanted to buy something across state lines. Think how complicated that would make shopping in malls across state lines!

Breakin' It Down

In England, counterfeiting was considered treason. A uniformity of money is crucial to the financial security of all Americans. Illegally printing money jeopardizes the economy, so counterfeiting is a punishable crime.

How Can I Make a Difference?

Find out more about the American dollar. Look up how much the dollar was worth in the early 1900s and compare it with the dollar's worth today. Compare its value with other forms of money from around the world. Learn more at www.usinflationcalculator.com.

What Has It Done For Me Lately?

The U.S. dollar unifies the states together. You can always count on your dollar being valid in every state in America.

The general principles on which the fathers achieved independence were the general principles of Christianity. I will avow that I then believed, and now believe, that those general principles of Christianity are as eternal and immutable as the existence and attributes of God.

—JOHN ADAMS, IN A LETTER TO THOMAS JEFFERSON

wikimedia.com, public domain

ARTICLE I
Section 8

Clauses 7–8

⁷To establish Post Offices and post Roads;

⁸To promote the Progress of Science and useful Arts, by securing for limited Times to Authors and Inventors the exclusive Right to their respective Writings and Discoveries;

The Bottom Line

Article I, Section 8, Clauses 7–8 give Congress the ability to establish post offices and promote arts, sciences, and new discoveries.

What Were They Thinking?

Our Founding Fathers never wanted America to end up like England. They wanted America to be the land of opportunity, and they started by keeping government out of the way of inventors.

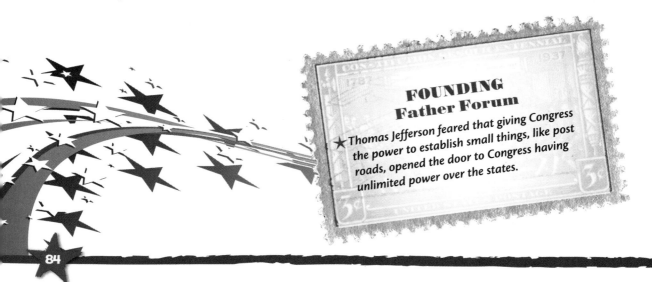

FOUNDING Father Forum

★ Thomas Jefferson feared that giving Congress the power to establish small things, like post roads, opened the door to Congress having unlimited power over the states.

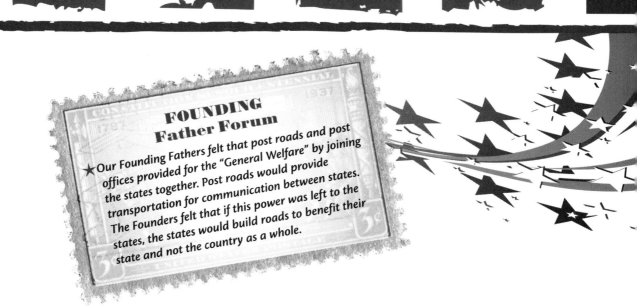

Why Should I Care?

Would you like it if the government censored every revolutionary idea you wrote down or every new invention you created? Thanks to this small clause in the constitution, we can create our inventions in peace without government intrusion.

Breakin' It Down

Clause 8 is the foundation of what made America great: freedom to reap the benefits of your own labor. Our Founders wanted people to be free to work and create, expanding the country and economy. This clause also grants Congress the ability to establish post offices across America.

OUR BRITISH ROOTS

In England, your work ended up in the king's hands and you never saw the benefits.

How Can I Make a Difference?

Do you have a friend or classmate at school that wants to grow up and become an inventor? Call them or talk with them next time you are at school and see if they know what clause in the Constitution protects their right to invent!

What Has It Done For Me Lately?

Without this clause in the Constitution, the government may have prevented Thomas Edison from inventing the light bulb! Other American inventions such as the airplane, tractor, traffic light, sewing machine, dishwasher, and much more could have been censored by the government and never created!

ARTICLE I
Section 8

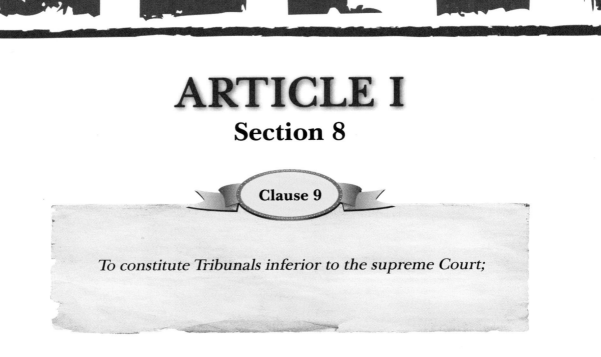

Clause 9

To constitute Tribunals inferior to the supreme Court;

The Bottom Line
Article I, Section 8, Clause 9 gives Congress the ability to create federal courts inferior to the Supreme Court.

What Were They Thinking?
When our Framers wrote this clause, they were giving Congress the sole power to create, ordain, and establish new federal courts throughout America that would hear legal cases throughout America. These courts would never supersede the powers of the Supreme Court.

Why Should I Care?
Let's say for example that you disagree with a federal law that was just passed (take, for example, the Affordable Care Act). You wouldn't take your case to a state court, but a federal court in your state. This court hears cases regarding bills passed by the U.S. Government. These are the courts that are set up by Congress, as stated in this clause.

LIBERTY Language

Federal Courts: A court that exercises jurisdiction over federal law – not state law.

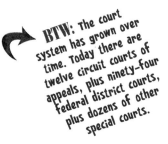

BTW: The court system has grown over time. Today there are twelve circuit courts of appeals, plus ninety-four federal district courts, plus dozens of other special courts.

Breakin' It Down

This clause gives Congress the ability to create other federal courts throughout America of different levels under the Supreme Court. It has a sister clause in Article III.

How Can I Make a Difference?

Knowledge is power! Do you know how many federal courts have been established since 1789? Find out at www.uscourts.gov.

What Has It Done For Me Lately?

In the current lawsuit on the Affordable Care Act, the states first had to sue the federal government through the federal courts across America which Congress had instituted through this clause. Thus, the institution of these courts is very important so that states' voices can be heard in our judiciary process.

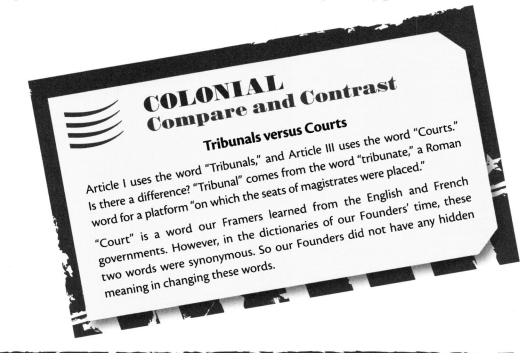

COLONIAL
Compare and Contrast

Tribunals versus Courts

Article I uses the word "Tribunals," and Article III uses the word "Courts." Is there a difference? "Tribunal" comes from the word "tribunate," a Roman word for a platform "on which the seats of magistrates were placed." "Court" is a word our Framers learned from the English and French governments. However, in the dictionaries of our Founders' time, these two words were synonymous. So our Founders did not have any hidden meaning in changing these words.

ARTICLE I
Section 8

Clauses 10–13

[10]To define and punish Piracies and Felonies committed on the high Seas, and Offences against the Law of Nations;

[11]To declare War, grant Letters of Marque and Reprisal, and make Rules concerning Captures on Land and Water;

[12]To raise and support Armies, but no Appropriation of Money to that Use shall be for a longer Term than two Years;

[13]To provide and maintain a Navy;

The Bottom Line

Article I, Section 8, Clauses 10–13 state that Congress has the ability to declare war, authorize private citizens to conduct military operations outside of the U.S., assemble and fund armies but for no longer than two years, and fund a navy.

What Were They Thinking?

Our Founding Fathers had been subject to kings or queens who could declare war at any time and make the people participate, so our Founders provided us with checks

FOUNDING
Father Forum

★ Our Founders were afraid if they gave war powers to the executive branch, the president would enter into a war without the people's consent. By giving the power to Congress, which represents the people and states, the Founders felt they compromised.

and balances by dividing the power of the military between Congress and the president. The president is commander-in-chief, but only Congress could declare and decide on the funding for war.

LIBERTY Language

Letters of Marque and Reprisal: A document issued by a nation allowing a private citizen to seize citizens or goods of another nation, or equip a private ship with arms in order to attack enemy ships.

Why Should I Care?

Since Congress has the power to declare war and send you or your loved ones into battle, it's important that our Constitution gives the people a say.

Breakin' It Down

These clauses outline congressional powers in wars and militia. Declaring war is one of the most important powers given to Congress. Only Congress can do it. (The president can't!) Congress can also punish pirates, and bizarrely, hire pirates to attack the nation's enemies. (A "Letter of Marque" is a letter that gives a pirate official permission to do his thing in the name of the national interest. Avast, ye mateys!)

The Founding Fathers were also really worried about the danger of standing armies, the kind of permanent professional armed forces that had been used by the British monarchy to oppress them before the Revolution. The Founders didn't want an army to stand for longer than was needed. To suppress the fear of a standing army, they established a maximum time limit for the funding of an army to two years.

How Can I Make a Difference?

Write a letter to a soldier fighting overseas and thank him or her for serving our country.

OUR BRITISH ROOTS

In Europe, only the king could declare war, and raise and support the armies.

What Has It Done For Me Lately?

In 2011, President Obama permitted American warplanes to participate in a NATO air strike, but Congress had not declared war against Libya or approved the invasion.

ARTICLE I
Section 8

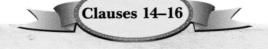

14 To make Rules for the Government and Regulation of the land and naval Forces;

15 To provide for calling forth the Militia to execute the Laws of the Union, suppress Insurrections and repel Invasions;

16 To provide for organizing, arming, and disciplining, the Militia, and for governing such Part of them as may be employed in the Service of the United States, reserving to the States respectively, the Appointment of the Officers, and the Authority of training the Militia according to the discipline prescribed by Congress;

The Bottom Line

Article I, Section 8, Clauses 14–16 establishes that Congress is in charge of declaring war and organizing and training the army and militia, which today is known as the National Guard.

What Were They Thinking?

Our Founding Fathers wanted a unified army, otherwise one state would be defending itself while another state would be defending itself. There would be no cooperation.

LIBERTY Language

Militia: Organized units of citizen soldiers. Today the militia has been replaced by the National Guard.

FOUNDING Father Forum

★ Our Founding Fathers knew their history, which is one reason our Constitution has remained standing and never faltered. Our Framers made a specific point to study past governments and learn from their mistakes.

Why Should I Care?

If we are attacked by an enemy, we want to be assured that we have a unified army to defend us.

Breakin' It Down

Our Founders did not want sole control of the military in the president's hands, and the states couldn't control the military by themselves because they would be too spread out and disorganized. Yet Congress could not have sole control. So who was left? They found their happy medium in a compromise between the president and Congress.

The president is commander-in-chief of our military, but to prevent tyranny, Congress must authorize the war and is responsible for funding it. Checks and balances.

Our Founding Fathers felt that if one body – such as the president – had sole power over the military, the chances would almost be inescapable that this one person would become a tyrant. If you look to the Republic of Rome, you see this in action; it was military control that threw Caesar into power. If you look at France you find the same military takeover put in play by Napoleon. Our Founders wanted to try to make sure that this tyrannical takeover would never occur in the United States.

How Can I Make a Difference?

Fighting for our country is an honor. Do you have a friend or family member who has served? Interview that person and write about their experiences.

What Has It Done For Me Lately?

The National Guard is a modern-day example of state militias. The National Guard operates as a backup to the U.S. Army, the difference being they are "state militias," but they can be called into action by the federal government if needed. Many National Guard units have served in Iraq and Afghanistan alongside the U.S. Army.

 BTW: Our army is sworn to protect the CONSTITUTION rather than the people, because the Constitution protects the people's freedoms.

ARTICLE I
Section 8

Clause 17

To exercise exclusive Legislation in all Cases whatsoever, over such District (not exceeding ten Miles square) as may, by Cession of particular States, and the Acceptance of Congress, become the Seat of the Government of the United States, and to exercise like Authority over all Places purchased by the Consent of the Legislature of the State in which the Same shall be, for the Erection of Forts, Magazines, Arsenals, dock-Yards, and other needful Buildings;

The Bottom Line

Article I, Section 8, Clause 17 is about where, why, and how the federal capital of the United States was to be established.

What Were They Thinking?

Our Founding Fathers wanted the capital of the United States to be a sovereign entity, so if a state ever decided to secede from the Union, like what happened in the Civil War, the capital would not go with it.

Why Should I Care?

It is important that the capital is its own entity so that it does not favor one state over another.

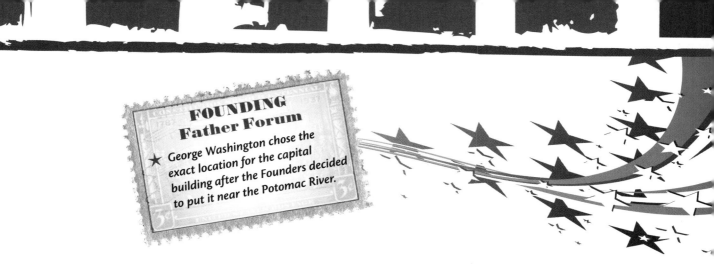

Breakin' It Down

During the Constitutional Convention, our Founding Fathers were considering two cities for the national capital: New York City and Philadelphia. So why is the capital not in one of those cities? Our Founding Fathers didn't want the federal government to be dependent on any state. Some wanted the federal government to be located in a "district," instead of a state. And some thought if the federal government controlled its own district without state supervision, it would be more prone to tyrannical control. Virginia and Maryland ended up giving some of their land to become what is now known as the District of Columbia.

Our Founders knew that people would live in this area, so they let D.C. have a state legislature for their local needs. After the Home Rule Act of 1973, D.C. was allowed a mayor.

On a related note, our Founders didn't think the government had the right to take land from the states for federal purposes, like national parks, but they allowed government to purchase state property as long as state's legislature agreed.

How Can I Make a Difference?

Teach your friends about the importance of having a sovereign capital.

What Has It Done For Me Lately?

There is a lot of debate today as to whether or not Washington, D.C. should become a state or merge with Maryland or Virginia. This would be totally against what our Founding Fathers intended and would call for major changes in our government, not to mention the United States flag. Because of the Constitution, it is, thankfully, not easy to transform D.C. into a state.

ARTICLE I
Section 8

Clause 18

To make all Laws which shall be necessary and proper for carrying into Execution the foregoing Powers, and all other Powers vested by this Constitution in the Government of the United States, or in any Department or Officer thereof.

The Bottom Line

Article I, Section 8, Clause 18 is known as the "Elastic," or "Necessary and Proper" Clause. It basically reinforces that Congress has the power to legislate, or create, laws – not the president or the courts.

What Were They Thinking?

Our Founding Fathers wrote this clause into the Constitution because they wanted to make sure the power of creating laws did not fall into the hands of a single person, the president, so they gave the power to Congress.

Why Should I Care?

This clause, like the rest of Article I, states that legislation is the job of Congress. However, some presidents claimed they could adopt rules and regulations to protect the economy and the environment if Congress failed to do so. This is an application of the Unitary Executive Theory, the theory that the president may apply separate constitutional powers in emergencies. This is very controversial.

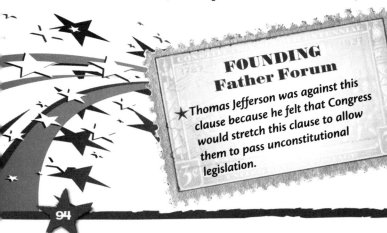

FOUNDING Father Forum

★ Thomas Jefferson was against this clause because he felt that Congress would stretch this clause to allow them to pass unconstitutional legislation.

> Congress are authorized to defend the nation. Ships are necessary for defense; copper is necessary for ships; mines, necessary for copper; a company necessary to work the mines....

> In other words, Congress would take their role of defending the nation and use that to take over, as Jefferson says, the shipping, copper, mining, and worker companies just because, they would say, all of that is used to defend the nation.

Breakin' It Down

This clause is known as the "Necessary and Proper" clause, and is the basis for all of the legislative branch's implied powers — powers not explicitly listed in the Constitution but held by Congress to be legitimate because they are "necessary and proper" for exercising other, listed powers. This clause was written to reinforce the idea that Congress is solely responsible for creating laws. Today, though, this clause has been used to justify a gradual expansion in the general power of Congress and the entire federal government — exactly what Jefferson warned about.

LIBERTY Language

Unitary Executive Theory: A doctrine put forth by Hamilton and many other presidents that states the president is head of the executive branch and has authority to interpret the Constitution independently of Congress and the Supreme Court.

> How do you think our Founding Fathers would feel about the Unitary Executive Theory?

How Can I Make a Difference?

Regularly watch the news. Be aware of recently passed laws and how they affect you.

What Has It Done For Me Lately?

In the Supreme Court case *U.S. v. Comstock,* Congress used this clause to justify its actions "to protect the public from dangers created by the federal criminal justice and prison systems." Is this one of Congress's jobs granted in the Constitution? Does this justify the fears of Thomas Jefferson?

ARTICLE I
Section 9

Clause 1

The Migration or Importation of such Persons as any of the States now existing shall think proper to admit, shall not be prohibited by the Congress prior to the Year one thousand eight hundred and eight, but a Tax or duty may be imposed on such Importation, not exceeding ten dollars for each Person.

The Bottom Line

Article I, Section 9, Clause 1 is known as the "Slave-Trade Clause," and prohibits the slave trade in the United States after 1808. It also allows Congress to enforce a small tax on the importation of slaves. Slavery itself was later abolished by Amendment Thirteen.

What Were They Thinking?

Our Founding Fathers needed a way to keep both the North and the South happy in regard to slavery in order to form a union and build a foundation of freedom which would eventually extend to all people.

FOUNDING Father Forum

★ Most of our Founding Fathers were against slavery.

Why Should I Care?

This clause was the first time the Constitution mentions an effort to abolish slavery. If our Founding Fathers had not established this clause in the Constitution, the slave trade might not have been prohibited by Congress until much later. This was the first major step in the right direction toward the abolition of slavery.

Breakin' It Down

"Such Persons as any of the States now existing shall think proper to admit" is a really long-winded way of saying "slaves" without actually saying "slaves." The Constitution barred any attempt to outlaw the slave trade before 1808. As soon as that date rolled around, Congress voted to block the international slave trade, although slaves continued to be sold within the country, and slavery itself lasted for almost another sixty years.

Convention Chat

Article I, Section 9, Clause 1, is the first major stepping stone to the abolition of slavery by the Constitutional Convention. During this convention, the debate over this clause spanned four days. In this short time, our Founding Fathers accomplished an almost impossible task: keeping both the North and South happy while working towards the end of slavery.

Convention Chat

Our Founding Fathers made the judgment that if they were to deal with the issue of slavery at the time of the Constitution, or incorporate the absolute abolition of slavery in the document, the South would never vote in favor, and our Constitution would never have been ratified. However, in this clause, our Founding Fathers made an important start.

After Congress passed the abolition of the slave trade in 1807, the question arose, "What was to happen to ships and slave cargo when they arrived in port?" Were the slaves to be freed upon arrival, or were they to go into slavery? This sparked a heated debate in the House of Representatives in 1807. The North won this battle in their amended proposal to free the slaves, at first only in the North, but then in all states.

"I will tell you what was done, and it gives me high pleasure, that so much was done… [B]y this article after the year 1808, the congress will have the power to prohibit such importation, notwithstanding the disposition of any state to the contrary. I consider this as laying the foundation for banishing slavery out of this country; and though the period is more distant than I could wish, yet it will produce the same kind of gradual change which was pursued in Pennsylvania."

JAMES WILSON

Our Founding Fathers understood if they tried to deal with the issue of slavery at the time of the Constitutional Convention, our Constitution would never have been ratified. However, this clause was a step in the right direction.

How Can I Make a Difference?

Find out how many of your friends know which American document actually ended the slave trade.

What Has It Done For Me Lately?

This clause proves our Founding Fathers wanted to end slavery, but they knew that they could not abolish it completely at this time. The South wouldn't ratify the Constitution if it abolished slavery.

ARTICLE I
Section 9

Clauses 2–3

²The Privilege of the Writ of Habeas Corpus shall not be suspended, unless when in Cases of Rebellion or Invasion the public Safety may require it.

³No Bill of Attainder or ex post facto Law shall be passed.

The Bottom Line
Article I, Section 9, Clauses 2–3 state that the right to habeas corpus cannot be denied to anyone unless they took part in rebellion or invasion.

What Were They Thinking?
In the days of our Founding Fathers, people in Britain were thrown into dungeons and jails without a warrant or justification of their crimes. Our Founders wanted to make sure this would never happen in America.

Why Should I Care?
The writ of habeas corpus prevents you from being held in jail without reason.

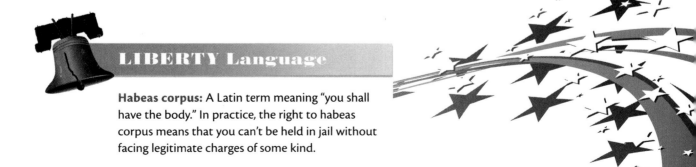

LIBERTY Language

Habeas corpus: A Latin term meaning "you shall have the body." In practice, the right to habeas corpus means that you can't be held in jail without facing legitimate charges of some kind.

Breakin' It Down

The writ of habeas corpus is perhaps the most important foundation of civil liberties. The right to habeas corpus means you can't be held in jail without facing legitimate charges of some kind, and that there is no such thing as indefinite detention without due legal process. A prisoner asks, or petitions, the court for the writ. If granted, the writ is given to the jailer for the prisoner's release.

In the days of the 19th century, this writ held such an essential role in our —judiciary system, that the federal courts could issue this writ even if Congress did not recognize the power. The Habeas Corpus Writ is a tool used to test the constitutionality of the detention of a prisoner. This writ is not used to judge if the person is guilty or innocent; rather, it is a "get out of jail card" for a prisoner if he pleas he is being held in jail unconstitutionally.

BTW: President Lincoln during the Civil War suspended the writ to a portion of Maryland. He then declared that the judiciary branch was inadequate to deal with organized rebellion. Lincoln's attorney general, Edward Bates, then claimed that this clause in the Constitution "did not specify which branch could suspend the writ, only the conditions under which it could be suspended."

OUR BRITISH ROOTS

The writ of habeas corpus – also known as the Great Writ – is traced, by some historians, back to the Magna Charta. However, this clause is more commonly traced back to the Habeas Corpus Act of 1679 under the reign of Charles II.

How Can I Make a Difference?

Many other countries today such as China and Syria imprison their citizens without any form of trial and without the writ of habeas corpus. Make sure your friends know about the importance of this clause in the Constitution.

What Has It Done For Me Lately?

During the Civil War, President Abraham Lincoln (in one of his most criticized moves ever) suspended habeas corpus. During the War on Terror, President George W. Bush controversially argued that terrorism suspects held at Guantanamo Bay, Cuba, had no right to habeas corpus and therefore could be held indefinitely without trial.

BTW: As of 2012, the Supreme Court is still ruling on the issue of habeas corpus in regard to detainees at Guantanamo Bay. In 2006, an act passed through Congress denied the detainees in Guantanamo the writ of habeas corpus. In a 5-4 opinion, the Supreme Court ruled this act unconstitutional.

ARTICLE I
Section 9

Clauses 4–6

⁴No Capitation, or other direct, Tax shall be laid, unless in Proportion to the Census or Enumeration herein before directed to be taken.

⁵No Tax or Duty shall be laid on Articles exported from any State.

⁶No Preference shall be given by any Regulation of Commerce or Revenue to the Ports of one State over those of another: nor shall Vessels bound to, or from, one State, be obliged to enter, clear, or pay Duties in another.

The Bottom Line
Article I, Section 9, Clauses 4–6 said no tax can be placed on citizens of a state unless the tax is based on population, no taxes could be placed on exports between the states, and no preference could be given to one state over another.

What Were They Thinking?
Our Founding Fathers wanted to establish a fair and uniform tax code in America, so they based it on population. However, they didn't want a state to be taxed on goods being imported from another state. They wanted to maintain free trade and harmony and give a sense of common purpose between states.

Capitation tax: Also known as a "poll tax" or "head tax," these taxes are a tax on individuals to help fund local needs, like roads and schools.

Convention Chat

Southern economies at the time of the Constitutional Convention depended upon the export of cash crops like cotton, tobacco, rice, and indigo.

Why Should I Care?

Today, if you buy something on the web from another state, there is no sales tax. This is because this clause in the Constitution prohibits tax on goods transferred from state to state. Thus, because of this clause, we can shop the web "sales tax free."

Breakin' It Down

Clause 4 states that Congress is not allowed to issue taxes unless they are based on the population. A capitation tax is a "head tax," one charged to each individual in the population. This clause required Congress to levy any taxes on the basis of a state's population, not on the basis of individual income or any other standard.

Though Congress has the power to tax imports, Congress can't charge taxes for shipping goods from one state to another, and it can't favor one state's ports over another—say with lower taxes. This clause was important to states like Maryland. Maryland-bound ships had to pass through Virginia ports in order to reach their final destination.

AMENDMENT Preview

The 16th Amendment, passed in 1913, struck the reference to "other direct Tax[es]," making it possible to create the modern personal income tax system that we know and love today.

How Can I Make a Difference?

Check labels on items you purchase, and try to buy items made in the USA.

What Has It Done For Me Lately?

Having no export tax makes items manufactured in the United States less expensive for sale overseas, which can ultimately help Americans get jobs because American businesses flourish as a result of lower prices.

ARTICLE I
Section 9

Clause 7

No Money shall be drawn from the Treasury, but in Consequence of Appropriations made by Law; and a regular Statement and Account of the Receipts and Expenditures of all public Money shall be published from time to time.

The Bottom Line
Article I, Section 9, Clause 7 says Congress must publish a record of all expenses paid out of the U.S. Treasury.

What Were They Thinking?
Our Founders felt that this clause would prevent Congress from drawing money from the Treasury unaccountably and would force them to become a little more prudent in their spending, since it was to be logged and published.

Why Should I Care?
Responsibility. We hear that a lot from our parents. But if we have to be responsible all the time, shouldn't our representatives in Washington be so also? This clause holds our representatives responsibile for the money they take

The first phrase in clause 7 can be traced back in history to England's Glorious Revolution where Parliament stated in the English Bill of Rights, that raising and levying money for the Crown without Parliament's consent is illegal.

from the U.S. Treasury. Congress must publish an account of the money they use. Congress's control over the government's money is perhaps the most important check against unlimited presidential power.

Breakin' It Down

This clause is critically important, granting Congress (and only Congress) the "power of the purse"—that is, control over government spending. The president can't get his hands on one dime of the public's money without Congress first approving all spending in an appropriations bill.

Money cannot be taken out of the National Treasury without Congress passing an appropriations bill. Meaning Congress has to pass a bill that allows the designated amount of money mentioned in the bill to be removed from the Treasury. There is debate on this first section of clause 7 about whether or not the president has authority to refuse to spend the money taken out of the treasury by the appropriations bill.

". . . And a regular Statement and Account of the Receipts and Expenditures of all public Money shall be published from time to time." This clause orders Congress to keep a log on all receipts and spending sprees of the public's money.

How Can I Make a Difference?

Research how much money our Congress spent out of the U.S. Treasury last year. Go a step further and see how the money was used. A helpful website for this is www.Thomas.gov. Would our Founding Fathers approve of the use of this money?

What Has It Done For Me Lately?

By ordering that our Congress keep a log of their expenses, it keeps our representatives accountable for all of the money they spend. With the amount of debt in 2012 at $15 trillion, it is as important as ever that our Congress keeps a log of every dollar that they spend.

The history of this clause can be traced way back to the time of Moses and the Israelites. This phrase in clause 7 is proof of biblical influence on the Constitution. In Exodus, "Moses himself came back after the construction of the Ark of the Covenant with a report on how the funds raised were actually spent."

ARTICLE I
Section 9

Clause 8

No Title of Nobility shall be granted by the United States: And no Person holding any Office of Profit or Trust under them, shall, without the Consent of the Congress, accept of any present, Emolument, Office, or Title, of any kind whatever, from any King, Prince, or foreign State.

The Bottom Line

Article I, Section 9, Clause 8 says no citizen of the United States can be given a title of nobility by the United States government. Also, no person in politics can be "kinged" or crowned with a noble title.

What Were They Thinking?

Our whole Revolutionary War was fought to protect America from ever having a "king" again. Our Founding Fathers fought that war for a nation that would abide under this clause. They wanted to make certain that no king or nobility would seize America.

Why Should I Care?

If any person was granted the title "king" in the United States, he could take over our republican form of government and strip us of our freedoms.

Who knew a title could mean so much?

Breakin' It Down

According to this clause, no title of nobility can be granted by the United States, and any political officer shall not receive the title of nobility from a foreign country without the consent of Congress. Also, presents are mentioned in this clause. Today, if you want to send a gift to a government official, it has to be under a certain price as a caution against bribery. As long as a gift is relatively cheap, it cannot be considered a bribe.

How Can I Make a Difference?

We hear about the appointment of "czars" by the president—and not the Russian kind. Even though they are not given an actual throne, they are still called "czars." Research czars and decide for yourself if you think they are constitutional. Find out under which president the practice of using czars began. Do they have powers that we don't want people to have in our republic form of government? If you decide against czars, send an email to the president's administration or your representatives asking them to reconsider the constitutionality of czars.

What Has It Done For Me Lately?

Would the current czars under the presidential administration be constitutional? The answer is no. A czar is a citizen that has ties to the president, and they are "insulated from the public," meaning they are not elected officials. However, they hold great power.

Russian Czar, Alexander II

ARTICLE I
Section 10

Clause 1

No State shall enter into any Treaty, Alliance, or Confederation; grant Letters of Marque and Reprisal; coin Money; emit Bills of Credit; make any Thing but gold and silver Coin a Tender in Payment of Debts; pass any Bill of Attainder, ex post facto Law, or Law impairing the Obligation of Contracts, or grant any Title of Nobility.

The Bottom Line

Article I, Section 10, Clause 1 establishes that no state can enter into an alliance with a foreign country, coin its own money, pay anything but silver and gold coins as payment for debt, or grant titles of nobility.

What Were They Thinking?

Our Founding Fathers wanted to make sure that the states remained *united* and did not become *too* independent.

Why Should I Care?

If each state was allowed to coin or print its own money, buying something in another state would be a serious hassle. If you tried to order something that was manufactured and sold in another state over the phone, you would have to convert funds through a bank first. And forget about ordering on the Internet!

Breakin' It Down

With this clause the Constitution places a small prohibition on the states. The phrase is like a small screw that holds a house together. If states were allowed to enter into agreements on their own, there would be a severe lack of unity among all the states and the name "United States of America" would mean nothing, for the states would become different entities, like in Europe.

This clause also deals with debt and money matters on the state level. We have learned that over the course of the war, the states had amassed separate debts. Later, all the debt was removed from the states and then given to the national government.

This clause also shows our Founders had little faith in paper money. Once again, their foresight proves legitimate. Today, our dollar has weakened, and gold and coin money has strengthened.

Also, the issue of nobility was already addressed on a national level in Section 9. This clause reiterates the point on a state level and proves the determination of our Founding Fathers.

> Separate countries with different money…

How Can I Make a Difference?

Compare the United States with Europe. If not for this clause, along with other sections of the Constitution, America would closely resemble Europe. Wouldn't that be a change?

What Has It Done For Me Lately?

We can take pride in the United States as a unified nation, working together, instead of a land mass made up of fifty different little countries.

ARTICLE I
Section 10

Clause 2

No State shall, without the Consent of the Congress, lay any Imposts or Duties on Imports or Exports, except what may be absolutely necessary for executing it's inspection Laws: and the net Produce of all Duties and Imposts, laid by any State on Imports or Exports, shall be for the Use of the Treasury of the United States; and all such Laws shall be subject to the Revision and Controul of the Congress.

The Bottom Line
Article I, Section 10, Clause 2 establishes that Congress, not the states, has the authority to tax imports and exports, and the funds from those taxes will be given to the U.S. Treasury.

What Were They Thinking?
Under the Articles of Confederation, instead of the government laying a uniform tax, each state had its own tax rules on imported and exported goods. Our Founding Fathers had no other choice than to take away the states' rights of laying taxes on imports and exports and placing that right and responsibility into the hands of the federal government.

Why Should I Care?
Without this clause, each state would have different regulations regarding taxes on imports and exports from foreign countries.

Let's say you lived in Kentucky and your friend lived in California. You both want to buy the same type of car for your sixteenth birthday. But this car is coming from Japan, and even though the cars are identical, you have to pay more money than your friend does because Kentucky has a higher tax rate. Not fair!

Breakin' It Down

This clause grants Congress the sole authority to lay taxes on imports and exports and gives profits from these taxes to the federal government. Without this clause, each state could have different import and export taxes. This would cause great confusion during Christmas shopping.

How Can I Make a Difference?

Having knowledge gives you power! Find out how much money Congress brings in each year because of the taxes they placed on imports and exports.

What Has It Done For Me Lately?

Trade is a large part of the American Economy. By taxing imports and exports, Congress brings in a steady flow of revenue. This clause is very applicable today due to America's constant involvement in world trade.

ARTICLE I
Section 10

Clause 3

No State shall, without the Consent of Congress, lay any Duty of Tonnage, keep Troops, or Ships of War in time of Peace, enter into any Agreement or Compact with another State, or with a foreign Power, or engage in War, unless actually invaded, or in such imminent Danger as will not admit of delay.

The Bottom Line

Article I, Section 10, Clause 3 says that states can't put taxes on tonnage, maintain a standing army, engage in agreements with countries or other states, or engage in war individually unless the state is attacked and in danger.

What Were They Thinking?

Our Founders wanted unity and security in times of war. They knew that a united country would stand stronger, which is also why they established one central army!

Why Should I Care?

Without this clause, the states could feasibly declare war on each other or other countries—essentially acting on their own rather than a unified country under one federal government.

Breakin' It Down

In this clause, our Constitution placed specific limitations on the states. States cannot lay taxes on tonnage – preserving

LIBERTY Language

Tonnage: Freight, and a ship's capacity for carrying freight.

Congress' commerce power. States cannot maintain a standing army – our Founding Fathers found a standing army would threaten the unity of the states as a whole, for example, if Missouri were to keep a standing army, the surrounding states would possibly feel threatened. States *are* allowed to maintain a militia, but states cannot engage in any agreements or treaties with foreign powers or other states. And states cannot engage in war individually, unless they are invaded or in imminent danger.

How Can I Make a Difference?

Read about your state Constitution and see how it parallels the U.S. Constitution.

Coming Full Circle with Shays' Rebellion

Shays' Rebellion was a movement by New England farmers who were desperate to be paid for their service in the Revolutionary War. Farmer Daniel Shays took charge of the group and led an attack on a federal arsenal in Springfield, Massachusetts, in January 1787. Massachusetts troops under Revolutionary War General Benjamin Lincoln came from Boston. Four men were killed and twenty wounded. Shays disappeared into the wilds of Vermont, not yet a state. Other men were arrested and imprisoned. Soon after, John Hancock was elected governor of Massachusetts. Hancock quieted everything down.

Shays' Rebellion illustrated two things:

- The national government under the Articles of Confederation was unable to raise money to pay back the debt or pay back the soldiers because Congress couldn't get states or individuals to give Congress money.

- Out of all this came a general agreement that a stronger federal government was needed. Later in 1787, the Constitution became a reality.

BTW: Massachusetts raised a temporary army in 1786 to deal with Shays' Rebellion.

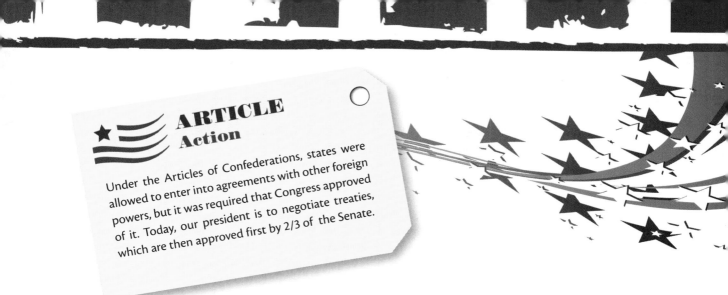

ARTICLE Action

Under the Articles of Confederations, states were allowed to enter into agreements with other foreign powers, but it was required that Congress approved of it. Today, our president is to negotiate treaties, which are then approved first by 2/3 of the Senate.

What Has It Done For Me Lately?

By establishing that states can only engage in war if directly attacked or in extreme, imminent danger, the Constitution preserves the state's right of self-defense.

We have now finished learning about Article I, the longest Article in the Constitution. Now onto Article II!

HAILING THE CHIEF
ARTICLE II
Section 1

Clause 1

The executive Power shall be vested in a President of the United States of America. He shall hold his Office during the Term of four Years, and, together with the Vice President, chosen for the same Term, be elected, as follows.

The Bottom Line

Article II is all about the executive branch. Article II, Section 1, Clause 1 established the second branch of government, made up of the president and vice president, elected together, every four years.

What Were They Thinking?

With the creation of the office of the president, our Founding Fathers created a government position unlike any other in the world. They wanted to make sure the president served as a check on other branches of government while never obtaining too much power.

Why Should I Care?

The office of the president is very important. As the youth of America, we have the responsibility of voting when we come of age, and it is extremely important for us to be informed voters when the time comes, so we can choose our president wisely and knowledgably.

ALEXANDER HAMILTON

Breakin' It Down

By granting the president a sweeping "executive power" —a power not carefully defined in the Constitution— Article II establishes the presidency as a strong office within the American government. That broad executive power gives the president the authority to enforce the country's laws created in Congress and administer the country's public policies. This clause also indicates that the president's (and vice president's) term of office lasts four years.

How Can I Make a Difference?

Choose one of your favorite presidents and learn more about him, like important legislation he vetoed or approved, and the name of his vice president.

What Has It Done For Me Lately?

Our nation's first African-American president, President Barack Obama, was elected in 2008.

A President versus a King

Some people in the time of the Constitutional Convention were afraid the president was too similar to a king. In order to persuade the people otherwise, Alexander Hamilton wrote the 69th Federalist Paper and listed some differences.

1. The president is only in power for as long as the people of the United States elect him. A king is in power for as long as he lives.

2. A president can be impeached for disorderly behavior, through a clean, civilized process – thanks to Congress. A king can rarely be punished without a national revolution.

3. A president retains executive power, but he rarely has the final say. If he vetoes a piece of legislation, Congress can override the veto. A king, however, contains absolute authority over his Parliament and Parliamentary legislation.

4. The president can only appoint officers and generals with the consent of the Senate. A king can create and appoint offices and officers without any consent of the Parliament.

5. Even though the president is known as "commander-in-chief," only Congress has the authority to declare war. A king has complete control and can enter into sieges and wars, create armies, and raise funds without anyone's consent.

 Pop Quiz! Remember, Congress has the authority to raise an army and raise funds, not the commander–in–chief.

6. A president can only make treaties with other countries with the advice and consent of the Senate. A king can create and agree on treaties completely on his own.

What answer shall we give to those who would persuade us that things so unlike [the President v. King] resemble each other? The same that ought to be given to those who tell us that a government, the whole power of which would be in the hands of the elective and periodical servants of the people, is an aristocracy, a monarchy, and a despotism.

THE mode of appointment of the Chief Magistrate of the United States is almost the only part of the system, of any consequence, which has escaped without severe censure or which has received the slightest mark of approbation from its opponents. The most plausible of these, who has appeared in print, has even deigned to admit that the election of the President is pretty well guarded. I venture somewhat further, and hesitate not to affirm that if the manner of it be not perfect, it is at least excellent.

Essentially, Alexander Hamilton was saying that the mode of operation for electing the president was working, because it had not fallen to corruption.

ALEXANDER HAMILTON

ARTICLE II
Section 1

Clause 2

Each State shall appoint, in such Manner as the Legislature thereof may direct, a Number of Electors, equal to the whole Number of Senators and Representatives to which the State may be entitled in the Congress: but no Senator or Representative, or Person holding an Office of Trust or Profit under the United States, shall be appointed an Elector.

For example, Texas currently has 34 electoral votes— the number of senators (2) plus the number of its representatives (32).

The Bottom Line

Article II, Section 1, Clause 2 created the Electoral College: a body of electors from each state, who vote for the president based on which candidate received the majority vote in their state. The number of electors appointed by each state equals the number of representatives in the House plus the number of senators.

BTW: The majority of electoral votes needed to elect the president is 270.

What Were They Thinking?

Our Founders wanted to prevent states with large populations, like Texas, New York, and California, from dominating the elections. These states still contain more electors than states like Wyoming or Montana, but the playing field is lowered from a gap of millions of votes, to a gap of only tens of votes. So even the smallest states have at least three electoral votes—two senators plus one representative.

Also, the identities of the electors are hidden until the last possible day, because our Founders wanted to ensure the electors wouldn't be bribed or corrupted to vote a certain way. So if senators and congressmen were allowed to be chosen as "electors," then the elected candidate would be indebted to every legislator who cast a favorable vote.

Why Should I Care?

Let's say you live in Wyoming, or a state with a smaller population. If it were not for the Electoral College, states like California and New York, which have large populations, would overwhelm your votes in national elections. That would not be fair to you or other people living in smaller states because their votes would never be recognized.

Breakin' It Down

Here the Framers established the Electoral College as a system for electing the president. Each state gets a number of electoral votes equal to its number of U.S. representatives, plus its two senators.

Many Americans believe that when they vote on Election Day they are voting directly for the candidate whom they want to become president. Actually, the president is elected by a group of electors called the Electoral College, representatives from each state, who vote for the candidate who received the majority vote in their state. Each state receives one elector for its federal congressmen and senators.

> Number of the state's federal House representatives + Number of the state's federal senators = Number of the state's electors.

Our Constitution leaves it up to the states to decide how they will appoint their electors. Each election is different depending on the state.

How Can I Make a Difference?

In the next upcoming presidential election, listen for mentions of the Electoral College, or "number of electors."

What Has It Done For Me Lately?

If you are ever watching the news and see a stadium full of people waving flags from every state, you are looking at footage from the convention and all the electors.

"Winner-takes-all": The standard mode of operation which most states follow, which means the Electoral College members will all vote for the same candidate: the candidate who received the most votes by the people in their state. For example, if the majority of California's voters choose Barack Obama, California's fifty-five Electoral College members will vote en mass for Obama. "Winner-takes-all."

Electorial College Elections

The Electoral College is still at the forefront of every presidential election campaign. After the Republicans and Democrats pick their nominees, those nominees will run against each other. During the general election campaign between the two nominees, there will be many polls and statistics about how many "electoral votes" each candidate has. That shows how important those electoral votes and the "Electoral College" are to elect the president.

ARTICLE II
Section 1

Clause 3

The Electors shall meet in their respective States, and vote by Ballot for two persons, of whom one at least shall not lie an Inhabitant of the same State with themselves. And they shall make a List of all the Persons voted for, and of the Number of Votes for each; which List they shall sign and certify, and transmit sealed to the Seat of the Government of the United States, directed to the President of the Senate. The President of the Senate shall, in the Presence of the Senate and House of Representatives, open all the Certificates, and the Votes shall then be counted. The Person having the greatest Number of Votes shall be the President, if such Number be a Majority of the whole Number of Electors appointed; and if there be more than one who have such Majority, and have an equal Number of Votes, then the House of Representatives shall immediately chuse by Ballot one of them for President; and if no Person have a Majority, then from the five highest on the List the said House shall in like Manner chuse the President. But in chusing the President, the Votes shall be taken by States, the Representation from each State having one Vote; a quorum for this Purpose shall consist of a Member or Members from two-thirds of the States, and a Majority of all the States shall be necessary to a Choice. In every Case, after the Choice of the President, the Person having the greatest Number of Votes of the Electors shall be the Vice President. But if there should remain two or more who have equal Votes, the Senate shall chuse from them by Ballot the Vice-President.

Liberty cannot be preserved without a general knowledge among the people.

JOHN ADAMS

Before the clause was amended, the electors all voted for two candidates. The votes were sent to Washington, counted by the VP, who declared the winner. But if one nominee did not receive the majority of electoral votes, or if there was a tie, Congress took over and voted from the top five candidates.

FOUNDING FATHER FORUM

★ Alexander Hamilton and Thomas Jefferson were great political rivals, but Hamilton backed Jefferson in the election of 1800.

The Bottom Line

Article II, Section 1, Clause 3 outlined the original method of electing the president and vice president—and turned out to have serious problems. Thankfully our Founders established the capability to amend, because this entire clause was changed after the presidential election of 1800.

What Were They Thinking?

Our Founding Fathers designed the Electoral College to prevent the public from being fooled by a candidate who could put on the charm and win popularity with the people, but who wouldn't make a good president. Alexander Hamilton, warned against "unqualified flatterers" who persuade the people with "promises of favors," or candidates basing their campaigns on "soaring, but empty, rhetoric."

AMENDMENT Preview

AMENDMENT 12 AND THE ELECTION OF 1800

The presidential election of 1800 turned into an Electoral College mess and demonstrated serious problems in the Constitution's original presidential election design. In 1800 — one of the most important elections in American history — Thomas Jefferson defeated the incumbent president, John Adams. But Jefferson finished in an Electoral College tie with Aaron Burr, Jefferson's vice-presidential running mate. The problem was that originally the Constitution called for each elector to cast *two* votes for his top two presidential candidates. Whoever finished first would become president, and whoever finished second would become vice president. But this system didn't account for the development of political parties. In 1800, Jefferson and Burr were running together as Democratic-Republican against Federalists John Adams and Charles Pinckney. When Jefferson and Burr finished in a tie, the election went for a vote in the House of Representatives. In the end, Alexander Hamilton convinced members of his own party to defer to the will of the people and allow Jefferson to become president, and the Twelfth Amendment was established to prevent this from happening again. Under the Twelfth Amendment, electors now cast separate ballots for president and vice president.

Why Should I Care?

In 1824, Congress elected John Quincy Adams president because no candidate had received the majority of electoral votes needed to win. Thankfully, our Founders had established a backup plan within our Constitution.

> [The Constitution] confines the electors to men of whom the people have had time to form a judgment, and with respect to whom they will not be liable to be deceived by those brilliant appearances of genius and patriotism, which, like transient meteors, sometimes mislead as well as dazzle.

Breakin' It Down

When creating the Electoral College system, our Founders wanted to avoid elections directly by Congress or state legislators. So they divided the power into three separate hands: the state legislatures appoint electors to the Electoral College; the Electoral College nominates their candidate based on the opinion of the people; and Congress serves as tiebreaker, or the "Backup Plan."

JOHN JAY

The creation of the Electoral College lowered the chances of corruption because it is made up of a select number of people who are less likely to be swayed by the "sweet talk" of political candidates, resulting in the election of the more qualified candidates. The Electoral College is also buffered from bribes and other tactics because each year the electors change. They also meet in their home states, preventing pressure and opinions from other states. And federal officials and federal officeholders are kept away from presidential electors, preventing any electors from having "friends" in Washington.

How Can I Make a Difference?

Teach your friends and family about the Electoral College, and explain to them how important it is to maintain our republican form of government. Find more information at www.archives.com

AMENDMENT Preview

The 12th Amendment changed the structure of the Electoral College. The Twelfth Amendment was ratified after the discovery of two problems. One, the presidency of John Adams (with Vice President Thomas Jefferson) clearly showed that presidents and vice presidents from opposing parties do not work well together. Two, when the election of 1800 was handed off to Congress due to a tie, the result was a damaging deadlock of political factions.

LIBERTY Language

Secede: To withdraw from an organization (as a religious communion or political party or federation).

FOUNDING FATHER FORUM

In Federalist Paper #68, Alexander Hamilton explained that the Electoral College prevented candidates from gaining power with "talents for low intrigue, and the little arts of popularity." One major backlash of electing a president who based their campaign and nomination on popularity is he wouldn't do what was best for the country but what would best advance his political standing. But through our Electoral College system, our election cycle is buffered from popularity-based elections, which can happen in other democracies.

What has it done for me lately?

After the electors place their vote for who they want as the new president of the United States, the votes are still to this day counted by the vice president in front of the Congress in early January.

ARTICLE II
Section 1

Clause 4

The Congress may determine the Time of chusing the Electors, and the Day on which they shall give their Votes; which Day shall be the same throughout the United States.

The Bottom Line
Article II, Section 1, Clause 4 puts Congress in charge of deciding what day the states will elect their electors and when they will meet to vote for president.

What Were They Thinking?
Our Founding Fathers wanted the state's job of electing electors to be mandatory. Since Congress established the date and time, the people can be assured the states won't ever "opt out" of selecting electors.

Why Should I Care?
Without this clause the Electoral College could have no set date of when to meet! That would be a problem because then they all couldn't assemble in their own states at one time in order to cast their votes. That would really back up our election system.

Breakin' It Down

This clause directed Congress to specify a date to elect the President of the United States. Congress chose "the first Monday after the second Wednesday in December ... at such place in each State as the legislature of such State shall direct."

How Can I Make a Difference?

Find out who the past electors have been in your state. Did they vote for the same presidential candidate for whom the people voted during the election?

What Has It Done For Me Lately?

Every four years, during a presidential election year, your state will elect a certain number of new electors to be counted in the Electoral College.

ARTICLE II
Section 1

Clause 5

No Person except a natural born Citizen, or a Citizen of the United States, at the time of the Adoption of this Constitution, shall be eligible to the Office of President; neither shall any Person be eligible to that Office who shall not have attained to the Age of thirty five Years, and been fourteen Years a Resident within the United States.

The Bottom Line

Article II, Section 1, Clause 5 lists the requirements for becoming president: you have to be a natural-born citizen, at least thirty-five years of age, and have lived in America for fourteen years.

What Were They Thinking?

Just like congressmen and senators, the president has his own set of requirements. Our Founding Fathers wanted the president to be born in the United States and to have lived in the U.S. for a minimum of fourteen years so that the loyalty of the president would be to America and America only. By requiring the president be older, our Founders also wanted him to be wiser and more experienced than the younger congressmen.

BTW: Life expectancy in our Founding Fathers' time was a lot less, so age 35 was more like age 50 to them.

127

Why Should I Care?

It is important that we know the Constitutional requirements for becoming president so we can evaluate each candidate, and in case we ever want to run for office.

Breakin' It Down

This clause listed the requirements for becoming the president of the United States.

1. The candidate has to be a natural-born citizen:

A natural-born citizen is just a fancy way of saying "born in the United States." There are two exceptions to this requirement. One exception that no longer applies is if the candidate was born before the ratification of the Constitution, which would make the candidate over 200 years old today and the oldest person to ever run for office. Under federal law, if both parents were natural-born citizens, the candidate could be born outside the U.S. and still be eligible.

2. The candidate must be thirty-five or older:

Thirty-five might seem young to be president, but in retrospect Alexander Hamilton was only thirty during the Constitutional Convention in 1787, and James Madison was thirty-five.

3. The candidate has to have been a resident of America for fourteen years:

Our founders wanted to insure that the candidate had lived in his mother country for at least fourteen years. However, it's not required to be fourteen consecutive years.

How Can I Make a Difference?

Learn more about your favorite past presidents at www.whitehouse.gov. How old were they when elected? Did they ever live overseas before becoming president?

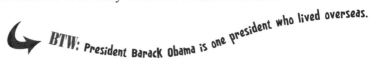

BTW: President Barack Obama is one president who lived overseas.

What Has It Done For Me Lately?

Our Constitution remains relevant after 225 years. All 46 of our presidents have been tested with these requirements—from today's president to George Washington!

ARTICLE II
Section 1

Clause 6

In Case of the Removal of the President from Office, or of his Death, Resignation, or Inability to discharge the Powers and Duties of the said Office, the Same shall devolve on the Vice President, and the Congress may by Law provide for the Case of Removal, Death, Resignation or Inability, both of the President and Vice President, declaring what Officer shall then act as President, and such Officer shall act accordingly, until the Disability be removed, or a President shall be elected.

The Bottom Line

Article II, Section 1, Clause 6 establishes that the vice president will take the place and duties of the president in the case of his death, resignation, or removal from office. If both the president and vice president are unable to serve, Congress will pass a statute specifying who will fill the vacancy until an election can take place.

What Were They Thinking?

Our Founders wanted to make sure that in case of the president's death, the transfer of power would be solved by the law, not by the sword.

Why Should I Care?

Nine vice presidents have assumed the presidency after the president died, resigned, or was assassinated. If our Founding Fathers had not written this clause into the Constitution, there would have been no backup plan, and the republic could have possibly fallen into the wrong hands.

Breakin' It Down

Two debates surround this clause. The first issue that arises is due to the small intricacies of the language of the Constitution. It's true if the president passes, resigns, or is unable to complete his duties, the vice president is next in line. But for how long? Was it our Founders' intent for the vice president to *become* the president, or just fill the job of the presidency until a special election takes place? This issue was resolved first by a precedent, and later an Amendment. President William Henry Harrison passed away in 1841, months after his inauguration. His vice president, John Tyler, assumed the presidency. Tyler was criticized for this action, but he created a precedent followed by future vice presidents: The VP becomes president for the remainder of the term, with all the powers of the president.

And what exactly did our Founding Fathers mean when they wrote "inability"? This question was tossed back and forth until 1967 when Amendment Twenty-Five stated the president could declare himself disabled, and resume his duties once recovered. *However*, if the president is unable or unwilling to recognize his disability, the vice president and the majority of his cabinet decide. If the president disagrees with his vice president and cabinet's decision, the ball is tossed into the Congress's court, and they decide the fate of the presidency.

How Can I Make a Difference?

Research an instance when a vice president had to assume the president's role at www.senate.gov. What happened? Was the vice president elected for a second term?

What Has It Done For Me Lately?

Gerald Ford was the last vice president to assume the office of the presidency after President Richard Nixon resigned in 1974. He fulfilled the last two years remaining in Nixon's term, but was not reelected.

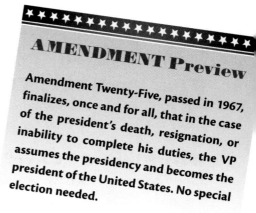

AMENDMENT Preview

Amendment Twenty-Five, passed in 1967, finalizes, once and for all, that in the case of the president's death, resignation, or inability to complete his duties, the VP assumes the presidency and becomes the president of the United States. No special election needed.

ARTICLE II
Section 1

Clause 7

The President shall, at stated Times, receive for his Services, a Compensation, which shall neither be encreased nor diminished during the Period for which he shall have been elected, and he shall not receive within that Period any other Emolument from the United States, or any of them.

The Bottom Line

Article II, Section 1, Clause 7 established a paycheck for the president. The president will receive a paycheck for his job but it cannot enlarge or decrease while he is in office and he cannot receive any bonuses.

What Were They Thinking?

Our Founding Fathers wanted the president to be able to provide for himself, yet they didn't want the president to be distracted from his job. Today, Congress has to pass a law to raise the president's salary. However, our Founders were concerned that if the Congress was allowed to raise the salary of the sitting president they would raise or lower his salary in order to make him more dependent upon Congress (like when parents raise or lower their child's allowance based on their behavior).

Why Should I Care?

We know our parents need paychecks in order to provide for the family. Our president needs to provide for his family as well and not worry about making ends meet while taking care of the nation. But it wouldn't be fair to the American taxpayers if he could raise his pay anytime he wanted.

Breakin' It Down

The president's salary is on a fixed rate, meaning it won't rise and fall during his presidency. It remains important that our president is paid from the U.S. Treasury and not any state because if one state funded the president's salary, that state would naturally seek a reward. The Constitution does not mention the payment of the vice president, but our Founding Fathers agreed to pay a small salary to the VP.

How Can I Make a Difference?

Look up how many times the president's paycheck has been raised and by how much. Do you agree with the amount the president is being paid or do you think it should be more or less?

What Has It Done For Me Lately?

The president of the United States is currently paid $400,000 a year for his service to the country. However, President George Washington was only paid $25,000 a year for his service to the country. While it sounds like the president today is being paid a royal salary, you should know that in Washington's time, gold was under $20 an ounce and today it is over $1,600 an ounce. Today the federal budget is 10,000,000 times that of the president's salary. In Washington's time the federal budget was 50 times the president's salary. Washington's pay today would be equivalent to $2,000,000!

FOUNDING Father Forum

★ Benjamin Franklin was opposed to the idea of a compensated president because he feared the desire for money would attract the wrong kinds of presidential candidates.

FOUNDING Father Forum

★ Our Constitution closely resembles the Massachusetts Constitution, written by John Adams in 1780, which included an article regarding the compensation (or salary) for an executive. It noted that the salary would prevent the executive from being distracted by benefactors or the need to earn money.

Generally indeed the ruling power carries its point, the revenues of princes constantly increasing, and we see that they are never satisfied, but always in want of more. The more the people are discontented with the oppression of taxes; the greater need the prince has of money to distribute among his partizans and pay the troops that are to suppress all resistance, and enable him to plunder at pleasure.

Convention Chat

Franklin's argument about presidential salary was paid no heed in the Constitutional Conventions. Why? Franklin had been the main architect of the failed Pennsylvania Constitution, and our Founding Fathers had learned not to trust Franklin. The clause passed with a unanimous vote.

BENJAMIN FRANKLIN

ARTICLE II
Section 1

Clause 8

Before he enter on the Execution of his Office, he shall take the following Oath or Affirmation:–"I do solemnly swear (or affirm) that I will faithfully execute the Office of President of the United States, and will to the best of my Ability, preserve, protect and defend the Constitution of the United States."

The Bottom Line

Article II, Section 1, Clause 8 said the president must take the oath of office, or oath of affirmation to follow the Constitution. The Clause actually spells out the exact language of the presidential oath of office, which must be taken upon the president's inauguration.

What Were They Thinking?

Our Founding Fathers wanted the president to recite an oath before entering office in which he would swear to defend the

FOUNDING Father Forum

★ President George Washington did not take the Oath of Office until April 30, over a month after he took office. George Washington was most likely just following the ways of his British roots, for the British Constitution does not require that the oath be taken instantly.

Constitution. Our Founders wanted to guarantee that the president would obey and protect the Constitution for future generations because the Constitution protects the people.

Why Should I Care?

It's important that the president's words match his actions. His words include the "Oath Of Office", so it's important we know what the oath says so we can hold the president accountable. Is he or she defending and protecting the Constitution like they promised?

Breakin' It Down

The president must faithfully execute his office and defend the Constitution and take care that the laws be faithfully executed. However, what happens if a current president refuses to defend a law because he believes it unconstitutional, even if it had been passed by a previous Congress and president? This instance occurred when President Obama announced he would not back the constitutionality of DOMA (the Defense of Marriage Act). This bill was passed by Congress, and signed by President Bill Clinton. So does President Obama have the right to reject the act, if it had already been constitutionally accepted?

How Can I Make a Difference?

See if your friends know the oath of office. Recite it for them.

What Has It Done For Me Lately?

When Supreme Court Chief Justice John Roberts flubbed the oath during Barack Obama's 2009 inauguration, mixing up the order of the words, Obama had to take the oath again in a private ceremony the next day, just to make sure that he was really president under the terms of the Constitution.

BTW: According to custom, the president recites the Oath of Office when he's first elected into office. His Oath of Affirmation needs only be recited once before the president "can execute the functions of his office." However, an old Venetian custom required when the new duke of Venice assumed power, the duke of Venice would recite the Venetian oath of office that explicitly described all the limitations of power that are placed on the new duke. Not only that, the Venetian oath of office was recited to the duke of Venice every two months, just as a reminder of his limitations of power.

THOMAS JEFFERSON

[Each branch of government] must have a right in cases which arise within the line of its proper functions, where, equally with the others, it acts in the last resort without appeal, to decide on the validity of an act according to its own judgment, and uncontrolled by the opinions of every other department.

He's suggesting that each branch was the sole interpreter of its constitutional powers. His theory implies that any questionable actions can be justified if a president says he did it because he had to uphold his oath of affirmation. So far the Supreme Court has not upheld Jefferson's view.

The President's Oath of Office

"I do solemnly swear (or affirm) that I will faithfully execute the office of president of the United States, and will to the best of my ability, preserve, protect and defend the Constitution of the United States."

LIBERTY Language

Oath of Office: A statement recited by the president upon his election stating that he will uphold the Constitution and be the best president he can.

Unappropriated: 1. Not granted to any person, corporation, or the like, to the exclusion of others; as, unappropriated lands. 2. Not granted for, or applied to, any specific purpose; as, the unappropriated moneys in the treasury.

BTW: The Oath of Office has been used by many presidents to justify their actions. Once, President Abraham Lincoln, after ordering two million dollars of unappropriated funds be paid out of the Treasury during the start of the Civil War, explained his actions as executing his duty to "preserve, protect, and defend" the Constitution by preserving the Union.

ARTICLE II
Section 2

Clause 1

The President shall be Commander in Chief of the Army and Navy of the United States, and of the Militia of the several States, when called into the actual Service of the United States; he may require the Opinion, in writing, of the principal Officer in each of the executive Departments, upon any Subject relating to the Duties of their respective Offices, and he shall have Power to grant Reprieves and Pardons for Offences against the United States, except in Cases of Impeachment.

The Bottom Line

Article II, Section 2, Clause 1 stated several important presidential powers. He is commander-in-chief of the military and state militias when they are called into service, and he has the power to pardon individuals convicted of federal crimes.

What Were They Thinking?

Our Founding Fathers saw how disorganized our Revolutionary War was with all the states acting as different countries, so the Framers established one solitary person who would be in charge of all the armies.

Why Should I Care?

It's important to know who is calling the shots when it comes to war. It's equally important to realize when electing someone into office, that he will be the sole person in charge of leading the army and navy in war.

Breakin' It Down

This clause explains how Congress is officially in charge of declaring war and raising funds for war, and the president is commander-in-chief of the war. However, there is an exception. If a foreign country attacks the United States first, the president can deploy troops without the consent of Congress. The president also has the power to pardon people accused of or convicted for federal crimes. However, a pardon doesn't prevent someone from being impeached by the House and removed by the Senate.

How Can I Make a Difference?

Take a survey next time you are at the grocery store with your parents and see if the people you run into know about the president's executive powers and his control of the armed forces.

What Has It Done For Me Lately?

There have been many upsets about this clause concerning the president's actions. A recent example was under the presidency of Ronald Reagan, when he invaded Lebanon by sending U.S. troops as a multi-national force to stabilize Lebanon during the evacuation of the Palestine Liberation Organization without consulting Congress beforehand.

The Constitution supposes, what the history of all governments demonstrates, that the executive is the branch of government most interested in war, and most prone to it. It has accordingly with studied care, vested the question of war in the legislature.

JAMES MADISON

ARTICLE II
Section 2

Clause 2

He shall have Power, by and with the Advice and Consent of the Senate, to make Treaties, provided two thirds of the Senators present concur; and he shall nominate, and by and with the Advice and Consent of the Senate, shall appoint Ambassadors, other public Ministers and Consuls, Judges of the supreme Court, and all other Officers of the United States, whose Appointments are not herein otherwise provided for, and which shall be established by Law: but the Congress may by Law vest the Appointment of such inferior Officers, as they think proper, in the President alone, in the Courts of Law, or in the Heads of Departments.

The Bottom Line

Article II, Section 2, Clause 2 gave the president the power to make treaties and appoint ambassadors, judges, and other officers—as long as the Senate approves.

What Were They Thinking?

In another demonstration of checks and balances, the Founding Fathers gave the president power to negotiate treaties and appoint people to positions, but only if the Senate approves.

Why Should I Care?

The government would be a very strange place if the president was allowed to appoint anyone he chose to a certain position. For example, imagine if a president appointed a news reporter as a judge to repay a favor? Fortunately, we don't have to worry because the Senate must approve all appointments.

Breakin' It Down

Clause 2 states that the president has the power to negotiate foreign treaties, but the Senate must concur by a two-thirds majority.

The president can also nominate men and women to aid him during his presidency, such as ambassadors. However, our Founders knew that if the president was left up to his own devices, he could nominate any citizen into a government job as a "favor," and corrupt the entire system. Our Founding Fathers found a cure by allowing the president to nominate his desired citizen to fill the job, but the Senate must approve the nominations by a majority vote, meaning the majority of senators present, yet there must be a quorum.

How Can I Make a Difference?

Do some research at www.senate.gov and see if you can find a statistic of how many presidential appointments the Senate has rejected. Take one example and look into the person of whom the Senate did not approve.

What Has It Done For Me Lately?

We have all heard the term "czar" in reference to the president's officials that he appoints, often without the consent of the people. These presidential jobs are exactly the type our Founding Fathers feared. These are appointed officials who are buffered from public opinion and thus have the ability to do as they choose without being accountable to "we the people."

LIBERTY Language

Czar: Top level officials appointed by a president that may not be approved by the Senate, and who can therefore influence policy unchecked.

ARTICLE Action

Under the Articles of Confederation, the delegates from the states were nominated to negotiate treaties, but this method left some states without representation for a long period of time. Our Founding Fathers fixed this issue by granting the president authority over treaty negotiations, but keeping senators in the loop by requiring a two-thirds concurrence, or agreement.

Those Crazy Czars!

Since the days of President Richard Nixon there have always been policy "czars."

- Ronald Reagan had three czars in eight years.

- George W. Bush had 14 czars in eight years.

- President Obama had 34 czars in just six months, nine are Senate approved (25 are not approved):

  - Deputy Interior Secretary David J. Hayes ("California Water Czar")
  - Director of National Drug Control Policy Gil Kerlikowske ("Drug Czar")
  - OMB Deputy Director Jeff Zients ("Government Performance Czar")
  - Director of National Intelligence Adm. Dennis Blair ("Intelligence Czar")
  - OMB Administrator of the Office of Information and Regulatory Affairs Cass Sunstein ("Regulatory Czar")
  - Assistant to the President for Science and Technology and OSTP Director John Holdren ("Science Czar")
  - Treasury Assistant Secretary for Financial Stability Herb Allison ("TARP Czar")
  - Assistant Secretary of Defense for Acquisition, Technology and Logistics Ashton Carter ("Weapons Czar")
  - OSTP Associate Director Aneesh Chopra ("Technology Czar")

FOUNDING Father Forum

★ Our Founding Fathers looked to Montesquieu's wisdom while writing the Constitution. Montesquieu wrote that the separations of power should not result in each branch of government being independent, but, instead, each branch should be dependent on each other. He stated that no department should "possess the whole power of another department."

ARTICLE II
Section 2

Clause 3

The President shall have Power to fill up all Vacancies that may happen during the Recess of the Senate, by granting Commissions which shall expire at the End of their next Session.

The Bottom Line

Article II, Section 2, Clause 3 said whenever an elected official leaves office unexpectedly, and the Senate happens to be at recess, the president is in charge of filling the vacant slot.

What Were They Thinking?

Our Founding Fathers wanted to make sure that if a vacancy occurred while the Senate was away, the seat would not remain empty until the next senatorial meeting. So they gave the president the power to fill the vacancies.

Why Should I Care?

It is important to know that the person we elect as president has the power to fill an empty seat in our government if the Senate is at recess. This appointed person can't serve more than two years unless the Senate votes to approve the nomination.

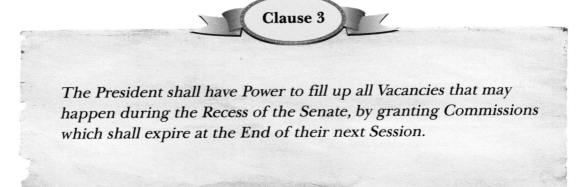

Breakin' It Down

What did our Founding Fathers intend when they used the words "vacancies"? If a federal official in the executive branch resigns from their office or dies, and our Senate happens to be on recess, the duty of "filling" the vacancy falls into the hands of the president. Filling vacancies are rather common in our legislative and executive branches; however, in our judicial branch, vacancies do not occur as often while the Senate is in recess.

The phrase "that may happen during the Recess of the Senate" means that the president only has this capability if the Senate is in recess.

The last phrase of clause three states that if our Senate does not approve a nomination by the president, the nominee can serve until the end of the legislative session but then must resign from power.

How Can I Make a Difference?

Knowledge is power! Research how many appointments have been made by the president during a Senatorial recess and compare them with the numbers of — appointments the Senate has reversed upon return. Check www.senate.gov.

What Has It Done For Me Lately?

An example of when this clause in the Constitution has come into play was when President Obama appointed a lawyer into a vacant slot on the National Labor Relations Board while the Senate was in recess.

BTW: When the Senate is in recess for such a short amount of time, like holiday weekends, or even a month-long break, the president would barely have the time to start putting in place a nomination, let alone officially nominate a citizen to a vacant slot in our federal government.

BTW: The most recent judicial "replacement" during a senatorial recess occurred under President George W. Bush, when he appointed two judges during a senatorial recess. President Bill Clinton nominated one judge, and before that, President Dwight D. Eisenhower appointed THREE Supreme Court justices, including a Chief Justice, during a senatorial recess.

ARTICLE II
Section 3

He shall from time to time give to the Congress Information of the State of the Union, and recommend to their Consideration such Measures as he shall judge necessary and expedient; he may, on extraordinary Occasions, convene both Houses, or either of them, and in Case of Disagreement between them, with respect to the Time of Adjournment, he may adjourn them to such Time as he think proper; he shall receive Ambassadors and other public Ministers; he shall take care that the Laws be faithfully executed, and shall Commission all the Officers of the United States.

The Bottom Line

Article II, Section 3 outlines specific presidential powers, including one of the president's most important duties—to make sure the laws of the United States are upheld.

What Were They Thinking?

If the powers were not specifically listed within the Constitution, then the branches of government would have unlimited powers. That's what "enumerated powers" means—numbered powers, as in limited. It was extremely important to the Framers to have limits on power and checks and balances in place on all branches.

Why Should I Care?

Having a president with limited, specific powers prevents us from living under a dictatorship.

Breakin' It Down

This section is a bit of a grab bag of various presidential duties. The president is required to report to Congress on "the State of the Union." Over time, this requirement has taken the shape of a formal "State of the Union Address" delivered every January to a joint meeting of both houses of Congress. The president can call Congress into special session when it's out on recess if he thinks there is urgent business the Congress needs to deal with. The president has to "faithfully execute", or enforce, the laws of the United States; this is probably the most important part of the presidential job description, so it's a bit odd that it's just tucked into the latter half of this clause. Finally, the president has to grant commissions, authority to act, to all military officers of the United States. See, it's a grab bag!

How Can I Make a Difference?

Tune in whenever the president holds a State of the Union address! Follow the White House on Twitter, @Whitehouse.

What Has It Done for me lately?

In the State of the Union address, the president outlines his plan for the country to Congress, but today's social media has provided all kinds of possibilities. In 2011, President Barack Obama held a "Twitter Town Hall," in which he answered questions from Twitter users for about an hour. He also held live, streamlined events on Facebook. This marked a whole new direction for the president to interact directly with the people and get feedback on his ideas and proposals.

I would love to know what our Founding Fathers would have thought about a Twitter Town Hall.

ARTICLE II
Section 4

The President, Vice President, and all civil Officers of the United States, shall be removed from Office on Impeachment for, and Conviction of, Treason, Bribery, or other high Crimes and Misdemeanors.

The Bottom Line

Article II, Section 4 confirmed that the president or vice president could be impeached for treason, bribery, or other crimes.

What Were They Thinking?

Our Founding Fathers created the power of impeachment because if the president knows he can be impeached, he will act more responsibly.

Why Should I Care?

The impeachment process is a very valuable aspect of our government. If we find that our president is not fulfilling his constitutional duties or commits a blatant act of treason against America, Congress can impeach him instead of having to wait until his term expires.

Breakin' It Down

After the House votes for impeachment (as we have learned before), the process goes to the Senate, where the senators vote on the impeachment charges against the president under the Chief Justice, who presides over the process.

Impeachment is used to discipline the president, vice president, or any governmental officer for disorderly conduct. However, what is disorderly conduct, exactly? In the Constitutional Convention, catch phrases were thrown out, such as "malpractice and neglect of duty" or "high crimes and misdemeanors." Our Founding Fathers still were more specific in their definition of an impeachable act by listing treason and bribery as two examples.

How Can I Make a Difference?

Make a diagram of the impeachment process. Show your friends and family and make sure they understand how vital this process is in maintaining our freedoms. Find information at www.senate.gov.

What Has It Done For Me Lately?

Two presidents have been impeached excluding Richard Nixon who resigned before the House voted to impeach him. No president has been convicted of a crime in a court of law. Other officers, however, have been impeached and removed from power.

★★

Presidential Impeachments

Of sixty-three attempts at impeachment, only nineteen have been impeached. Of those, eight have been convicted after trial by the Senate. Because it cripples the Senate with a lengthy trial, impeachment is infrequent. Many officials, seeing the writing on the wall, resign rather than face the ignominy of a public trial. The most famous of these cases is of course that of President Richard Nixon, a Republican. President Richard Nixon resigned from office rather than suffer impeachment proceedings in the Watergate scandal in 1974. President Bill Clinton became the second president to be impeached by the House in 1998. Later, the Senate found him not guilty.

Our 17th president, Andrew Johnson, was impeached while in office. Thirty-five senators found him guilty — just one vote short of the two-thirds vote necessary to convict him.

Debate

Read the actual words spoken by our Framers.

The President of the United States would be liable to be impeached, tried, and upon conviction of treason, bribery, or other high crimes and misdemeanors, removed from office; and would afterwards be liable to prosecution and punishment in the ordinary course of law. The person of the King of Great Britain is sacred and inviolable: There is no constitutional tribunal to which he is amenable, no punishment to which he can be subjected without involving the crisis of a national revolution.

Alexander Hamilton makes the point that the president can be removed from office for bad behavior, while the King of Great Britain has no legal consequences for bad behavior. This must be one reason why it's good to be the King.

ALEXANDER HAMILTON

Benjamin Franklin wanted to keep the impeachment clause, and thought it would be better for the executive to be accountable and punished for bad behavior, even removed from office, because this gave him the opportunity to make amends. The alternative, according to Franklin, could be assassination. I think I'd rather be impeached.

History furnishes one example only of a first magistrate being formally brought to public justice. Every body cried out against this as unconstitutional. What was the practice before this, in cases where the chief magistrate rendered himself obnoxious? Why, recourse was had to assassination, in which he was not only deprived of his life, but of the opportunity of vindicating his character. It would be the best way, therefore, to provide in the Constitution for the regular punishment of the executive, where his misconduct should deserve it, and for his honorable acquittal, where he should be unjustly accused.

BENJAMIN FRANKLIN

HERE COMES THE JUDGE! THE JUDICIAL POWER
ARTICLE III
Section 1

Clause 1

The judicial Power of the United States, shall be vested in one supreme Court, and in such inferior Courts as the Congress may from time to time ordain and establish. The Judges, both of the supreme and inferior Courts, shall hold their Offices during good Behaviour, and shall, at stated Times, receive for their Services, a Compensation, which shall not be diminished during their Continuance in Office.

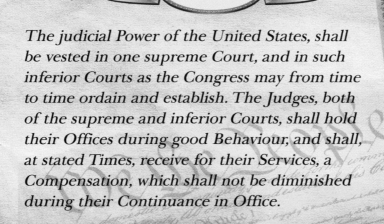

The Bottom Line

Article III, Section 1, Clause 1 established our judicial branch, the Supreme Court of the United States, and granted Congress the power to establish inferior federal courts. The Supreme Court is the head of the judicial branch in the same way the president is the head of the executive branch.

What Were They Thinking?

Our Founding Fathers established the Supreme Court to serve as a check for the other two branches of government, to judge the laws created by Congress, and also to serve as the final judges for court cases.

Why Should I Care?

The Supreme Court is the third branch of our government and the highest court of the land. If a lower level court makes an unconstitutional or questionable ruling, the people have the right to appeal to a higher court. Also, without the Supreme Court, our president and Congress could pass laws without being checked by another branch of government. With the Supreme Court, we can rest assured that Congress cannot get away with passing unconstitutional laws.

Breakin' It Down

Article III established the Supreme Court and allowed Congress to establish lower, inferior courts. The Supreme Court's main job is to make sure that the laws passed by Congress are constitutional. Federal judges are appointed for life terms and paid salaries that can't be cut during the time they remain on the bench.

The first Congress originally designated six justices to sit on the Supreme Court, but the number has risen to nine over the years. Our Founding Fathers didn't set a fixed number of justices because they expected the Supreme Court and the number of justices to increase as America grew. President Franklin Roosevelt unsuccessfully tried to increase the number of justices to benefit his own political program.

The Framers tried to plan for every slight mishap. By leaving the number of Supreme Court justices up to the current Congress, they gave Congress a pull on the direction of our Supreme Court.

The president appoints the Supreme Court justices with the consent of the Senate, but the number of justices that sit on the Supreme Court is up to Congress. (Checks and balances!)

How Can I Make a Difference?

Spread the word to your friends about the importance of the judicial system. Also, find out more about Sandra Day O'Connor, the first female Supreme Court justice.

What Has It Done For Me Lately?

Over 225 years of American history, Congress has established nearly 100 federal district courts, a dozen circuit courts of appeals, and several other types of special courts.

FOUNDING Father Forum

★ John Locke and Baron de Montesquieu are two philosophers whose theories greatly influenced our Founders as they built the cornerstones for our Supreme Court.

Judiciary Acts

The Judiciary Act of 1789 set by Congress established that the Supreme Court would have "five associate justices and one chief judge." It also established circuit courts, which have the original jurisdiction, meaning they hear the cases for the first time. Also under this act, Supreme Court justices had to "ride the circuit," meaning they had to serve on both the Supreme and circuit courts.

The Judiciary Act of 1891 overrode the previous act and set up this system: district courts hear all federal cases, issues where the U.S. is a party, or challenges to the constitutionality of a law. The circuit courts have appellate jurisdiction; and the Supreme Court hears only exceptionally important cases.

BTW: The Supreme Court was originally located in the basement of the Merchant Exchange Building in NYC and later in the U.S. Capitol. Not until President Taft did the Supreme Court receive its own individual building.

FOUNDING Father Forum

★ Our Founders felt that the judicial branch was "peripheral in the political process," meaning it was not center on the stage of importance.

FOUNDING Father Forum

★ President George Washington had a difficult time finding citizens to fill the slots for Supreme Court justices because citizens of the day felt that state officers, or circuit court judges, were of higher importance than the Supreme Court.

ARTICLE III
Section 2

Clause 1

The judicial Power shall extend to all Cases, in Law and Equity, arising under this Constitution, the Laws of the United States, and Treaties made, or which shall be made, under their Authority;–to all Cases affecting Ambassadors, other public Ministers and Consuls;–to all Cases of admiralty and maritime Jurisdiction;–to Controversies to which the United States shall be a Party;–to Controversies between two or more States;–between a State and Citizens of another State;–between Citizens of different States,–between Citizens of the same State claiming Lands under Grants of different States, and between a State, or the Citizens thereof, and foreign States, Citizens or Subjects.

The Bottom Line
Article III, Section 2, Clause 1 establishes which cases the Supreme Court is to hear.

What Were They Thinking?
Our Founding Fathers wanted to prevent small town court skirmishes from going straight to the Supreme Court.

Why Should I Care?
The Supreme Court's main job is to decipher the constitutionality of the laws passed by Congress and the president. Without the Supreme Court, unconstitutional laws could be passed and could significantly invade your personal freedoms.

Breakin' It Down

This clause describes in detail the world of our federal court system. It states which cases go to our federal courts—federal courts being either the Supreme Court or other inferior federal courts created by Congress. The Supreme Court is to hear cases involving laws and treaties of the United States, cases in which the U.S. is a party, cases involving two or more states, and cases between citizens from different states.

The Supreme Court or other federal courts rarely hear cases that do not fall under these guidelines. Other cases must go through local and state courts.

How Can I Make a Difference?

Find how many federal laws have been found unconstitutional by the Supreme Court.

What Has It Done For Me Lately?

In the time of our Founding Fathers, *diversity jurisdiction*—cases between citizens of different states—were more significant than *federal question jurisdiction*—cases that involved federal statutes. Today this has flipped: there are few cases that involve lawsuits between citizens from different states and more federal question cases.

Court Conversations

Since the Constitution enumerates the powers of the federal judiciary system, our federal courts have limited jurisdiction, meaning they can only hear cases approved by Congress or cases that the Constitution itself allows them to hear.

Our Founders created America's court system as a *decentralized* court system, meaning that any state and federal court can decide constitutional questions. In other words, judicial power is not just in one person's hands, rather the Constitution makes sure that judicial power is distributed among many different judicial bodies. Again, checks and balances!

Pop Quiz! Enumerated Powers=listed powers. Listed powers=limited powers. If the powers weren't specifically listed within the Constitution, the judicial system could have UNLIMITED powers.

Debate

Read the actual words spoken by our Framers.

The complete independence of the courts of justice is peculiarly essential in a limited Constitution. By a limited Constitution, I understand one which contains certain specified exceptions to the legislative authority ... Limitations of this kind can be preserved in practice no other way than through the medium of the courts of justice, whose duty it must be to declare all acts contrary to the manifest tenor of the Constitution void. Without this, all the reservations of particular rights or privileges would amount to nothing.

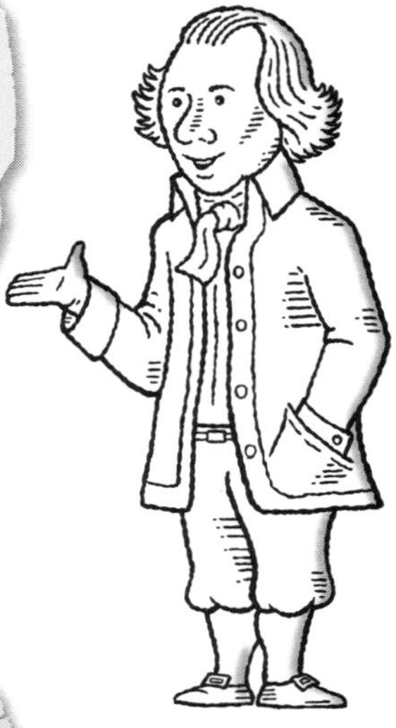

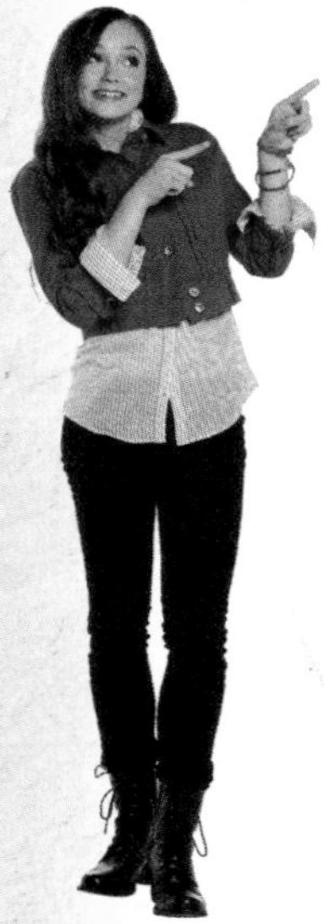

ALEXANDER HAMILTON

It's important to note that a judge's ruling on a constitutional matter, even though the people should respect the ruling, doesn't make that judge's opinion higher than the Constitution itself.

The supreme court under this constitution would be exalted above all other power in the government, and subject to no control...The judges are supreme and no law, explanatory of the constitution, will be binding on them.

He's arguing that the courts need to be independent of Congress, so the courts can void any unconstitutional laws. Without a way to declare laws unconstitutional, the entire Constitution would be pointless.

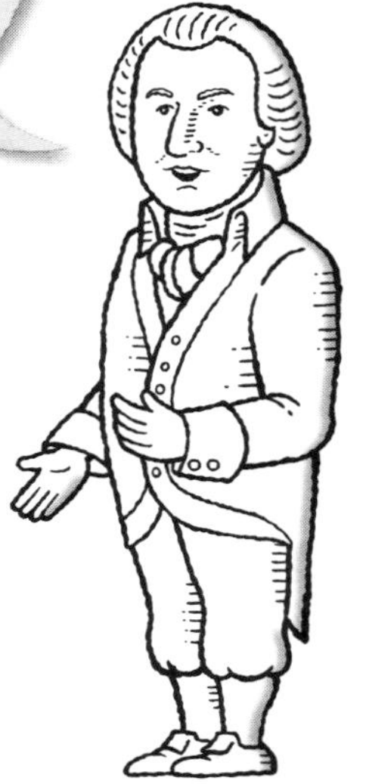

ROBERT YATES

He's arguing there aren't enough checks on the courts.

The interpretation of the laws is the proper and peculiar province of the courts. A constitution is, in fact, and must be regarded by the judges, as a fundamental law. It therefore belongs to them to ascertain its meaning as well as the meaning of any particular act proceeding from the legislative body.

ALEXANDER HAMILTON

The job of the courts is to interpret the laws, so it makes sense for the Supreme Court to make sure all laws are constitutional. The Constitution trumps all other law.

When great and extraordinary powers are vested in any man, or body of men, which in their exercise, may operate to the oppression of the people, it is of high importance that powerful checks should be formed to prevent the abuse of it ... I suppose the supreme judicial ought to be liable to be called to account, for any misconduct, by some body of men, who depend upon the people for their places.

ROBERT YATES

The opinion which gives to the judges the right to decide what laws are constitutional and whatnot, not only for themselves in their own sphere of action but for the legislature and executive also in their spheres, would make the judiciary a despotic branch.

Jefferson wrote this shortly after the Marbury v. Madison ruling of 1803, a landmark case that established the U.S. Supreme Court's right of judicial review.

THOMAS JEFFERSON

ARTICLE III
Section 2

Clause 2

In all Cases affecting Ambassadors, other public Ministers and Consuls, and those in which a State shall be Party, the supreme Court shall have original Jurisdiction. In all the other Cases before mentioned, the supreme Court shall have appellate Jurisdiction, both as to Law and Fact, with such Exceptions, and under such Regulations as the Congress shall make.

The Bottom Line

Article III, Section 2, Clause 2 said the Supreme Court should try cases involving ambassadors, public ministers, and states; and the Supreme Court also has appellate jurisdiction over other cases.

What Were They Thinking?

The Framers wanted to ensure a fair trial to everyone, including states! Our Founding Fathers wanted to make sure every legal dispute had a specific court and would receive a fair and unprejudiced trial.

LIBERTY Language

Appellate jurisdiction: The ability of the Supreme Court to review the rulings of other inferior courts, such as district and circuit courts.

Why Should I Care?

It's important to know how the judicial system works. If you're ever tangled up in a court case, you need to know whether you have the right to take your case to the Supreme Court if you do not agree with the verdict.

Breakin' It Down

This clause established that all legal disputes involving a state, ambassador, or other high-ranking diplomats, can be taken to the Supreme Court for trial.

What kind of dispute would affect an ambassador? Imagine a Chinese ambassador to America gets on a plane with someone from North Carolina, and the ambassador drops his briefcase on the person's toe and gets sued. The Supreme Court would decide this legal dispute, because the Chinese ambassador would not want to go to a North Carolina court, and it would be impossible to take the court case to China!

How about a state dispute? Let's say Nebraska sues Texas over price fixing of corn. Nebraska would want to take the issue to the Nebraska state courts, because a court in their home state would be more likely to rule in favor of the home state. Texas would want to take the issue to a Texas court for the same reason. Instead, the dispute would go directly to the Supreme Court.

If you're just an everyday citizen in the state of Oklahoma in a dispute between you and another everyday citizen in the state of Oklahoma, you don't receive that free pass to the Supreme Court. An everyday citizen must take his or her dispute to their statewide court.

How Can I Make a Difference?

Research a trial in your area that was appealed to the Supreme Court at www.supremecourt.gov.

What Has It Done For Me Lately?

Approximately 10,000 cases are appealed to the Supreme Court each year, but the Supreme Court only hears seventy-five to eighty of these cases. In 2012, the Supreme Court heard the appeals on the constitutionality of the Affordable Care Act of 2010.

ARTICLE III
Section 2

Clause 3

The Trial of all Crimes, except in Cases of Impeachment, shall be by Jury; and such Trial shall be held in the State where the said Crimes shall have been committed; but when not committed within any State, the Trial shall be at such Place or Places as the Congress may by Law have directed.

The Bottom Line

Article III, Section 2, Clause 3 preserves our right to a trial by jury and a trial within the state in which the crime was committed.

What Were They Thinking?

Right to trial by jury was suspended by Britain before the Revolutionary War, along with many other rights protected by this clause. Our Founding Fathers wanted to ensure trials took place in the state in which the original crime was committed in order to prevent the federal government from dragging us from state to state or trying people in secret. Our Founders wanted to protect the accused.

Why Should I Care?

Your right to a fair trial by jury will always be protected by this clause. Without this clause, our court systems could be corrupted, and innocent people wrongly convicted on a daily basis.

Breakin' It Down

This clause protects your right to be tried by the members of your local community. Plea bargaining is an option for an accused criminal when he is before a court, and an agreement is reached without a jury, even though the Constitution says that all trials of crimes shall be decided by jury. Plea bargaining has not been found to be unconstitutional, but that does not mean it isn't. The argument is plea bargaining is not forced upon any accused person, rather, it's simply a choice.

Though if you read the clause literally, you find our Founders thought a jury trial to be the best way to justice. So by plea bargaining are we actually abandoning the original intentions of our Founders? Or are we just taking a shortcut?

How Can I Make a Difference?

See if you have a juvenile court in your community and learn more about your local courts. Become involved!

What Has It Done For Me Lately?

A debate taking place today is in regard to the treatment of suspected terrorists. One side of the argument is that terrorists were arrested as enemy combatants (enemies of the military), and that the rights protected by the Constitution only apply to American citizens. The other side of the argument is that these rights apply to anyone under the control of American officials. But then the question is, how does one determine who is an enemy combatant?

ARTICLE III
Section 3

[1] Treason against the United States, shall consist only in levying War against them, or in adhering to their Enemies, giving them Aid and Comfort.

[2] No Person shall be convicted of Treason unless on the Testimony of two Witnesses to the same overt Act, or on Confession in open Court. The Congress shall have Power to declare the Punishment of Treason, but no Attainder of Treason shall work Corruption of Blood, or Forfeiture except during the Life of the Person attainted.

The Bottom Line

Article III, Section 3, Clauses 1-2 defines treason and the punishment for traitors.

What Were They Thinking?

Treason was an infamous issue among our Founding Fathers, and they wanted to make sure that they made their country as "treason-proof" as possible. The Framers took treason seriously. It was the one and only crime specifically defined in the Constitution, and it is mentioned seven times in the Constitution.

FOUNDING Father Forum

★ It is a big deal to be disloyal to one's own country. Our Founding Fathers knew this, and they intended to punish an American citizen who committed treason. However, they had to be careful. British monarchs used treason as a way to convict innocent people and just make them "disappear."

Why Should I Care?

This section protects you from the enemies of America, the people who betray our country. Also our Founders took great care that no one could easily be wrongly convicted.

Breakin' It Down

Our Founders viewed treason to be an act of war against the United States, or an act of aiding her enemies. Traitors are convicted by confession in front of a court or by two witnesses. Congress decides punishment against the traitor, but the traitor's family is protected, which is what the "Corruption of Blood" statement means. This is what our first United States congress regarded as just punishment: "If any person or persons, owing allegiance to the United States of America . . . shall be thereof convicted on confession in open court, or on the testimony of two witnesses to the same overt act of the treason whereof he or they shall stand indicted, such person or persons shall be adjudged guilty of treason against the United States, and shall suffer death."

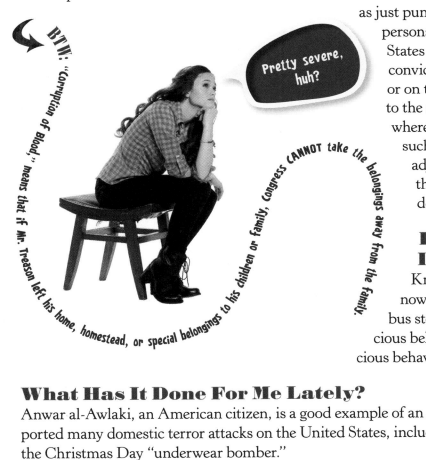

BTW: "Corruption of Blood," means that if Mr. Treason left his home, homestead, or special belongings to his children or family, Congress CANNOT take the belongings away from the family.

Pretty severe, huh?

How Can I Make a Difference?

Knowledge is power! Many cities now post signs in public places, like bus stops and airports, to report suspicious behavior. Keep an eye out for suspicious behavior.

What Has It Done For Me Lately?

Anwar al-Awlaki, an American citizen, is a good example of an American traitor. He has supported many domestic terror attacks on the United States, including the Fort Hood shooting and the Christmas Day "underwear bomber."

ACTING NEIGHBORLY
ARTICLE IV
Section 1

Full Faith and Credit shall be given in each State to the public Acts, Records, and judicial Proceedings of every other State. And the Congress may by general Laws prescribe the Manner in which such Acts, Records and Proceedings shall be proved, and the Effect thereof.

ARTICLE Action

Our Founding Fathers expanded this clause from one in the Articles of Confederation.

The Bottom Line

Article IV, Section 1, the "Full Faith and Credit Clause," establishes that each state has to recognize laws, records, and court rulings of other states.

What Were They Thinking?

Our Founding Fathers wanted to ensure that the states would work together in order to easily resolve legal issues.

LIBERTY Language

Litigate: To carry on a lawsuit

Why Should I Care?

If you ever get in a lawsuit against another individual, you want to know the same laws apply if one of you moves. Say your college roommate steals your car and then moves to another state. (It's just an example, don't worry.) You wouldn't be happy if you couldn't take legal action to get the car back because of different state laws.

Breakin' It Down

This section is known as the "Full Faith and Credit Clause." This clause is very important in keeping our states *United* — in regard to the judicial system. Each state in America has its own court system. For example, if a lawsuit arises in the state of North Dakota between Joe James and Deborah Doe, the case would be heard by the North Dakota court system. Thanks to this section, if Joe moved to Minnesota during the case, the Minnesota and North Dakota judicial systems would work together instead of starting over and re-litigating the entire case.

How Can I Make a Difference?

Surf the web and find some examples of when this section of the Constitution has come into play in your state. Share your findings with your friends and teach them about this clause.

What Has It Done For Me Lately?

This section in the Constitution has been debated today in regard to gun licenses. Let's say you lived in Texas and obtained a gun license to carry that gun on you at all times. When you travel to, say, New York – a state that does not permit those kinds of gun licenses – should you be arrested for carrying a gun, or should you be allowed to carry a gun because you have a Texas license?

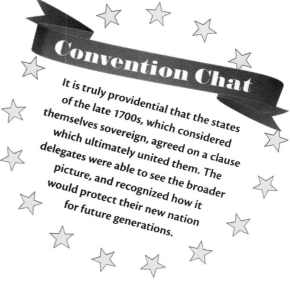

Convention Chat

It is truly providential that the states of the late 1700s, which considered themselves sovereign, agreed on a clause which ultimately united them. The delegates were able to see the broader picture, and recognized how it would protect their new nation for future generations.

Debate

Read the actual words spoken by our Framers.

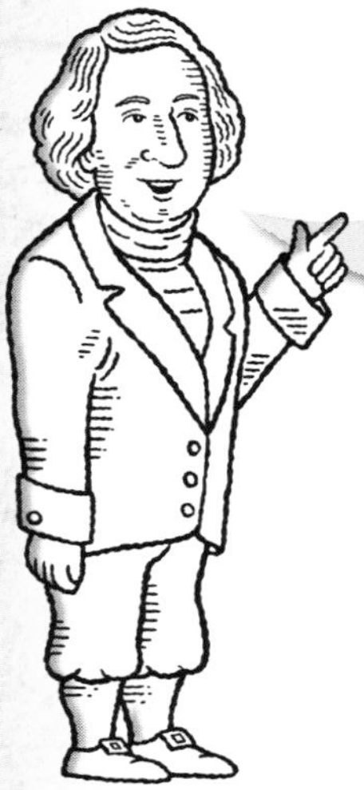

EDMUND RANDOLPH

Whenever the Act of any State, whether Legislative, Executive or Judiciary shall be attested & exemplified under the seal thereof, such attestation and exemplification, shall be deemed in other States as full proof of the existence of that act--and its operation shall be binding in every other State, in all cases to which it may relate, and which are within the cognizance and jurisdiction of the State, wherein the said act was done.

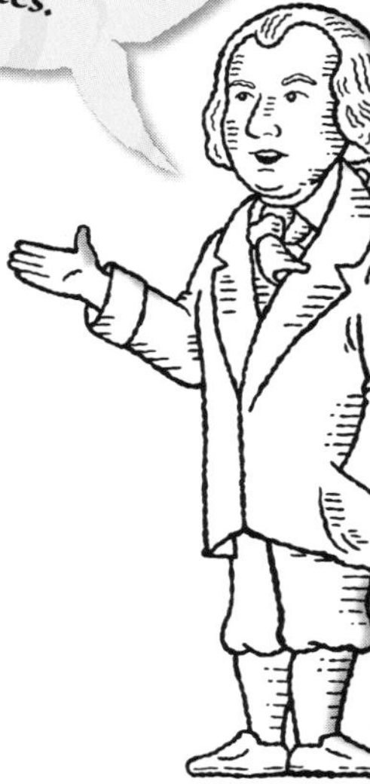

JAMES MADISON

This may be rendered a very convenient instrument of justice, and be particularly beneficial on the borders of contiguous States.

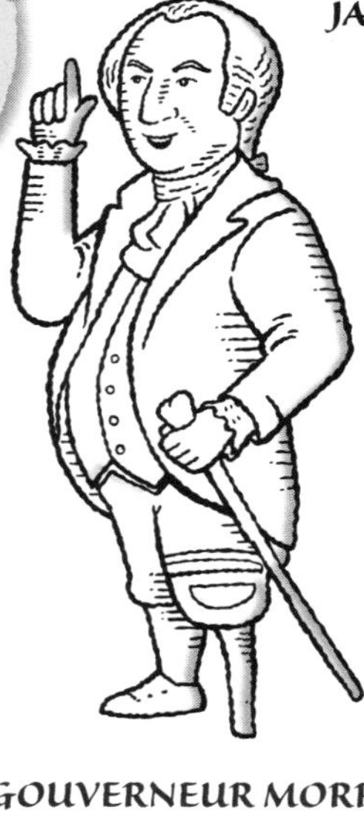

GOUVERNEUR MORRIS

Full faith ought to be given in each State to the public acts, records, and judicial proceedings of every other State; and the Legislature shall by general laws, determine the proof and effect of such acts, records, and proceedings.

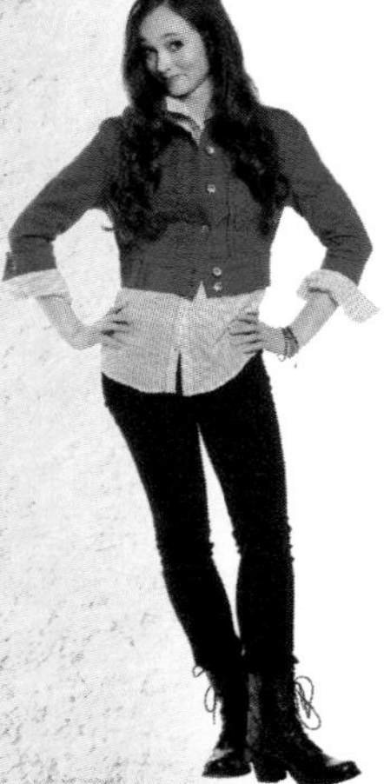

Gouverneur Morris is saying here that the states ought to have open communication with one another so that we may be the UNITED States of America.

ARTICLE IV
Section 2

Clauses 1–3

¹*The Citizens of each State shall be entitled to all Privileges and Immunities of Citizens in the several States.*

²*A Person charged in any State with Treason, Felony, or other Crime, who shall flee from Justice, and be found in another State, shall on Demand of the executive Authority of the State from which he fled, be delivered up, to be removed to the State having Jurisdiction of the Crime.*

³*No Person held to Service or Labour in one State, under the Laws thereof, escaping into another, shall, in Consequence of any Law or Regulation therein, be discharged from such Service or Labour, but shall be delivered up on Claim of the Party to whom such Service or Labour may be due.*

The Bottom Line

Article IV, Section 2, Clause 1, the "Privileges and Immunities Clause," says states can't discriminate against citizens from other states;

Article IV, Section 2, Clause 2, the "Extradition Clause," says states that capture fugitives from another state must send them back to face trial; and

Article IV, Section 2, Clause 3, the "Fugitive Slave Clause," said slaves who escaped into freedom in the North were required to be sent back to their owners in the South.

What Were They Thinking?

Our Founding Fathers wanted to assure citizens that their rights would not change when traveling from state to state. They also did not want criminals running rampant around the United States in order to escape punishment!

Why Should I Care?

Through Article IV, we can rest assured that our fundamental rights are protected whenever we drive or fly across state lines.

Breakin' It Down

Looking first at clause 2, the Extradition Clause was intended to prevent criminals from seeking refuge in another state. However, after a 1861 Supreme Court ruling, state governors were allowed to refuse requests for extradition, when justice so demands.

Clause 3 is known as the Fugitive Slave Clause. The Fugitive Slave Clause was used to prohibit northern states from protecting slaves who had escaped to freedom. Thankfully, this was repealed by the 13th Amendment.

Clause 1 is known as the Privileges and Immunities Clause, and it has had some controversy associated with it. This clause was meant to protect the rights of citizens traveling from state to state, but it has been interpreted four different ways.

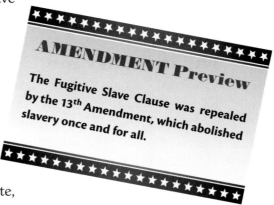

AMENDMENT Preview

The Fugitive Slave Clause was repealed by the 13th Amendment, which abolished slavery once and for all.

1. View One: Our Founders intended this clause to restrict Congress from passing discriminating laws against certain states and its citizens. This interpretation is constitutionally invalid today.

BTW: The lack of a judiciary in the Articles of Confederation became a problem because it was cumbersome to settle disputes between states.

2. View Two: This clause guaranteed that citizens of one state could enjoy the rights of citizens of other states. This meaning was rejected by the Supreme Court over a century ago.

3. View Three: This clause ensured the right of a citizen to exercise his state's rights when visiting another state — also rejected by the Supreme Court.

4. View Four: Our Founders intended this clause to prohibit discrimination against citizens from other states. For example, if a state permits its people to own land, it can't deny Johnny, a man from another state, to buy, say, vacation property in that state. This is the view upheld by the Supreme Court.

View four of the Privileges and Immunities Clause has been constitutionally accepted as the true, intentioned definition of this clause.

How Can I Make a Difference?

Find out more about the 1861 Supreme Court ruling and decide for yourself whether or not you believe that it was unconstitutional.

What Has It Done For Me Lately?

Article IV, Section 2 ensures that if someone injures you in your home state of Alabama and then flees to Colorado, then the Colorado governor must turn over the fugitive to the Alabama governor, if asked to do so.

ARTICLE IV
Section 3

Clauses 1–2

¹New States may be admitted by the Congress into this Union; but no new State shall be formed or erected within the Jurisdiction of any other State; nor any State be formed by the Junction of two or more States, or Parts of States, without the Consent of the Legislatures of the States concerned as well as of the Congress.

²The Congress shall have Power to dispose of and make all needful Rules and Regulations respecting the Territory or other Property belonging to the United States; and nothing in this Constitution shall be so construed as to Prejudice any Claims of the United States, or of any particular State.

The Bottom Line
Article IV, Section 3, Clauses 1–2 allows new states into the Union.

What Were They Thinking?
Our Founding Fathers wanted an easy way for new states to enter into the Union, so the United States could continue to grow.

Why Should I Care?
Without this clause, your state may never have been admitted into the Union, or your state could have been divided into smaller states, or America might still consist only of the original thirteen states. Talk about crowded!

Breakin' It Down

This clause lays the framework for the process of admitting states into the Union. The Framers of the Constitution planned for the future growth of the country, so they set up a system that allowed new states to be formed on the western frontier and enter the Union as equals to the original states. A state had to be admitted by Congress, and any territory not yet accepted as a state fell under congressional power. However, Congress couldn't take a piece of an existing state or join two states without the existing state's consent.

How Can I Make a Difference?

Find out how and when your state was admitted into the Union.

What Has It Done For Me Lately?

This clause prevents Congress and elected officials from taking a hold of your state and splitting it into smaller states or joining it with other states to benefit their own needs.

Early State Scenarios

- There has been some rule breaking. In 1791 during George Washington's presidency, Vermont became a state. Vermont had previously been a territory claimed by both New York and New Hampshire. However, Vermont had been self-governing for fourteen years.

- Kentucky was originally a group of western counties of Virginia that wanted to become a separate state.

- Of course, slavery eventually played a role in the annexation of states. Congress, from the 1790s to the 1860s, paired states when they were admitted. Why? Congress wanted to keep the national legislature balanced by admitting one pro-slavery state and one abolitionist state. When Congress admitted Missouri, a pro-slavery state, they had to also admit an abolitionist state. However, the north part of the country was booked up. To continue the balance of power, Congress split the northern portion off Massachusetts to create a new state, Maine. Massachusetts, agreeing with Congress's action to balance power, agreed to lose a large portion of their state.

- During the Civil War, West Virginia did not want to join Virginia in seceding from the Union. So the representatives from the counties revolted against their mother state, gathered in Wheeling, Virginia, and decided to become a state of their own called West Virginia.

- After breaking off from Mexico, Texas became "The Republic of Texas." Later, Texas wanted to join the United States. After consulting with Congress, Texas became a part of the Union. Did you catch the snag? This went against the established procedure because Texas was not a territory first! However, this was not unconstitutional, just out of the ordinary.

ARTICLE IV
Section 4

The United States shall guarantee to every State in this Union a Republican Form of Government, and shall protect each of them against Invasion; and on Application of the Legislature, or of the Executive (when the Legislature cannot be convened) against domestic Violence.

The Bottom Line

Article IV, Section 4 ensures states would always be ruled by a "Republican Form of Government," and the federal government would protect any state from foreign enemies, domestic violence, revolts, and rebellions.

What Were They Thinking?

Our Founding Fathers wanted to ensure that a republican government ruled both our states and our nation.

FOUNDING Father Forum

★ The Founding Fathers knew they had to leave enough powers with the states if they were going to ratify the Constitution. All states were granted the right to control certain things within their borders. They could do so as long as they did not interfere with the rights of other states or the nation.

Why Should I Care?

Our states could be attacked any day, and it is our national government's job to protect all of the states from foreign invasions. This protects us from communism, socialism, dictatorship, or a monarchy ruling our states.

Breakin' It Down

Our Founding Fathers voiced that they wanted to insure a "Republican Form of Government" to every state. Each state must maintain a republican form of government; no state is allowed to become a dictatorship. Also, the federal government promised to protect all the states from foreign military attack, and to come to the aid of any state threatened by uprisings or insurrections.

How Can I Make a Difference?

Remind your friends that without this section in the Constitution, your state could be ruled by a dictator instead of a governor or become socialist. Thanks to the Constitution, our country and states are republics.

What Has It Done For Me Lately?

This section assures that we are protected every day from invasion, revolt, and rebellion and that freedoms and republicanism are protected.

COLONIAL Compare and Contrast

In addition to their exclusive powers, national and state governments share certain powers, such as collecting taxes, building roads, borrowing money, establishing courts, making and enforcing laws, chartering banks and corporations, spending money for the general welfare, and taking private property for public purposes—with fair compensation.

CHANGING THE CONSTITUTION
ARTICLE V

The Congress, whenever two thirds of both Houses shall deem it necessary, shall propose Amendments to this Constitution, or, on the Application of the Legislatures of two thirds of the several States, shall call a Convention for proposing Amendments, which, in either Case, shall be valid to all Intents and Purposes, as Part of this Constitution, when ratified by the Legislatures of three fourths of the several States, or by Conventions in three fourths thereof, as the one or the other Mode of Ratification may be proposed by the Congress; Provided that no Amendment which may be made prior to the Year One thousand eight hundred and eight shall in any Manner affect the first and fourth Clauses in the Ninth Section of the first Article; and that no State, without its Consent, shall be deprived of its equal Suffrage in the Senate.

The Bottom Line

Article V enables the Constitution to be amended by the people's representatives as needed.

What Were They Thinking?

Our Founding Fathers wanted to instill a method for the American people to amend the Constitution whenever a significant majority thinks it's necessary because they knew they couldn't address everything.

Why Should I Care?

This article gives We the People power! Instead of having a governing document that can never be touched or altered, like in other countries, our Constitution is a document that can be changed by the people (as in you and me) so that it is for the people (that is, you and me).

Breakin' It Down

Article V gives the people a process by which to seek an amendment to the Constitution when they deem it necessary. How? Two ways. By getting their state to seek a constitutional convention or by getting a congressional representative to introduce the proposed amendment.

Our Founding Fathers knew the Constitution would need to be changed, eliminating slavery is one example, so the Founders established a way to make amendments without demolishing the whole document. Our Framers wanted unity, but they didn't want a complete paralysis of the amendment process like had happened under the Articles of Confederation. At the same time, the Framers wanted to prevent the amendment process from being too easy, in case radicals gained control of Congress.

The Constitution can be amended in two different ways: the first by the states who call together a constitutional convention; the second by Congress, who creates the amendment and then sends it to the states.

How Can I Make a Difference?

Don't take amendments for granted! The amendment process is one of the miraculous designs of our Constitution. Our Founding Fathers knew that the Constitution was an imperfect document, so they gave the people the ability to change the Constitution through amendments. Understand the amendment process.

COLONIAL Compare and Contrast

Unlike the English "Bill of Rights of 1689" which is unwritten and can be altered as if it is any other day-to-day legislation passed by British Parliament, our Constitution not only clearly describes the checks and balances of our government and the protection of America's citizens in writing, it also leaves a clear-cut path on which America can amend any portion of the document.

What Has It Done For Me Lately?

In addition to the Bill of Rights, the Constitution has been amended seventeen times since its creation to include such things as the eradication of slavery, women's right to vote, and much, much more.

The option of the national constitutional convention has been mainly avoided due to the fear that, if a national constitutional convention was to arise, the Constitution as a whole could be amended and significantly altered, as happened in 1787 at the Philadelphia Convention.

ARTICLE Action

It was extremely difficult, if not impossible, to amend the Articles of Confederation—one of many flaws. Similar to the "charter-like" way of the British, the Articles of Confederation could only be amended if all the states agreed.

The Amendment Process

The Constitution can be amended, or changed, through a formal process established by the Framers in 1787. First an amendment must be officially proposed by a two-thirds vote in both houses of Congress (or by two-thirds of all state legislatures), then it needs to be ratified by three-fourths of the state legislatures or the same number of state constitutional conventions. This process is difficult but not impossible to complete; over the course of American history, 27 different amendments to the Constitution have been ratified.

However, Article V included two restrictions upon amendments. The first restriction barred any amendments that would have outlawed the slave trade before 1808. And the second restriction ensured that no amendment could end the system of equal representation of all states, large and small, in the U.S. Senate.

OUR BRITISH ROOTS

Before the Revolutionary War, American colonists were ruled by British law under royal charters. Charters created a "legal" relationship between the Crown and the colonies. Any local laws within the colonies were only valid if they corresponded with the British charters. The colonist considered the charters "legitimate laws" because they were written, fundamental, and not amendable by ordinary legislation. Having a written charter was considered very important to the legitimacy of the document because signing a written charter bound all participants to the document. Charters were fundamental because they organized how the political process would run in the new colonies.

LAW OF THE LAND
ARTICLE VI

Clauses 1–3

¹All Debts contracted and Engagements entered into, before the Adoption of this Constitution, shall be as valid against the United States under this Constitution, as under the Confederation.

²This Constitution, and the Laws of the United States which shall be made in Pursuance thereof; and all Treaties made, or which shall be made, under the Authority of the United States, shall be the supreme Law of the Land; and the Judges in every State shall be bound thereby, any Thing in the Constitution or Laws of any State to the Contrary notwithstanding.

³The Senators and Representatives before mentioned, and the Members of the several State Legislatures, and all executive and judicial Officers, both of the United States and of the several States, shall be bound by Oath or Affirmation, to support this Constitution; but no religious Test shall ever be required as a Qualification to any Office or public Trust under the United States.

The Bottom Line

Article VI establishes four things: The new government under the Constitution would honor its past obligations; federal laws would be supreme over state laws (the supreme law of the land); elected officials would swear to uphold and protect the Constitution; and no religious tests would ever be required for any elected officials.

OUR BRITISH ROOTS

In Britain, the "Test Act" of 1672 required all public officers to swear an anti-Catholic oath renouncing the sacrament of the Lord's Supper.

What Were They Thinking?

Our Founding Fathers wanted America to have credibility, for the Constitution to have power, and for all government officials to honor the Constitution because the Constitution protects the people.

Why Should I Care?

Article VI made the Constitution the supreme law of the land and guaranteed its protection for future generations. Without this article, our representatives would not have to swear to protect the Constitution. As a result, they would not have to be accountable to the Constitution as well as the people!

Breakin' It Down

This Article contains the Supremacy Clause, the Oath Clause, and the No Religious Test Clause. First, this article guarantees the new government under the Constitution would still fulfill its money obligations, past, present, and future. This maintained U.S. credibility and credit.

The Supremacy Clause establishes the Constitution as the "supreme law of the land." In other words, laws passed by our national government that abide by the Constitution override state laws. However, *all* laws must abide by the Constitution!

If we mean to have those appointed to public offices, who are sincere friends to religion, we, the people who appoint them, must take care to choose such characters; and not rely upon such cob-web barriers as test-laws are.

OLIVER ELLSWORTH

The Oath Clause requires that all government officials swear to uphold the Constitution upon entering office. Though officials must swear by this oath, they will never be required to swear any oath to any religious affiliation—the No Religious Test Clause. Wouldn't it be horrible if the government made a law that only people from a certain religious denomination could serve as an elected official?

How Can I Make a Difference?
Make sure your elected officials know their Constitution when passing laws. You can do this by sending an email or letter to his or her office and by knowing the Constitution itself!

What Has It Done For Me Lately?
Over the last few years, the court has found that the Supremacy Clause is not violated when a state allows people to sue cigarette companies, even though the national government regulates cigarette advertisements.

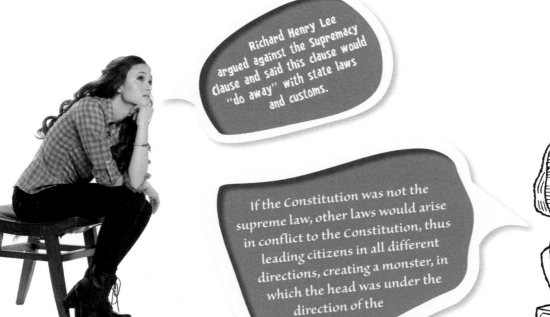

Richard Henry Lee argued against the Supremacy Clause and said this clause would "do away" with state laws and customs.

If the Constitution was not the supreme law, other laws would arise in conflict to the Constitution, thus leading citizens in all different directions, creating a monster, in which the head was under the direction of the members.

JAMES MADISON

MAKING IT OFFICIAL
ARTICLE VII

The Ratification of the Conventions of nine States, shall be sufficient for the Establishment of this Constitution between the States so ratifying the Same.

FOUNDING
Father Forum

★ George Washington was the first president under the Constitution, but there had actually been fourteen presidents before him, under the Articles of Confederation.

The Bottom Line

Article VII, the last in the Constitution, describes how this document, the United States Constitution, was to be ratified, or approved, by the states after its completion.

What Were They Thinking?

Our Constitutional Founding Fathers knew from experience that to obtain a unanimous consent from all the states, as the Articles of Confederation had required, would simply write "doom" over their hard work. It would be impossible to persuade all thirteen states to ratify the constitution, especially Rhode Island, who didn't send any delegates to the convention.

Why Should I Care?

Without this short clause, the Constitution may have never been ratified, and we wouldn't have a unified and productive government with such things we take for granted, like interstate highways, the protection of our armed forces, our three separate branches of government, an effective president, and the dollar bill.

Breakin' It Down

Article VII called for only nine out of the thirteen states to ratify the Constitution, allowing some buffer room around Rhode Island. New Hampshire was the ninth state to ratify the Constitution on June 21, 1788, preceding Virginia and New York, who slowly ratified by the end of July. Washington was elected president, a new Congress was elected, and the Constitution was set in place on April 30, 1789, despite the fact that North Carolina and Rhode Island had not yet ratified the new law of the land.

ARTICLE Action

America had functioned as an independent country for thirteen years before the Constitution was ratified. Before then, the U.S. had been governed by the Articles of Confederation, which could only be changed if Congress and the legislatures of every state agreed.

In 1789, that time had arrived.

How Can I Make a Difference?

Read the Constitution. See how many of your friends know how the Constitution was ratified. Get them to read the Constitution, too! Be sure to check out the Constituting America website and join the annual forums on the Constitution. Also, enter the We The People 9.17 Contest for kids at www.constitutingamerica.org. Prizes include a trip to Philadelphia and a starring role in a documentary. Categories range from a song, short film, public service announcement, essay, drawing, or poem, all about what the Constitution means to us today.

What Has It Done For Me Lately?

Because of this Article, our Constitution came into existence.

Convention Chat

Congress was the brain behind the Constitutional Convention. Congress was the one to call the convention into being, by summoning that each state send delegates to Philadelphia to "simply abridge" the Articles of Confederation. "For the sole purpose of revising the articles of Confederation and reporting to Congress and the several legislatures such alterations and provisions therein as shall, when agreed to in Congress and confirmed by the States, render the federal Constitution adequate to the exigencies of government and the preservation of the Union."

Little did those delegates know the momentous task ahead of them, or the miracle they would accomplish, when they created the United States Constitution.

THE AMENDMENTS
Twenty-Seven Amendments

In Article V, we learned that our Founding Fathers left us with a process by which we could amend our Constitution. Though not part of the original document, the Amendments have been incorporated into the Constitution, and they are just as important. In addition to protecting our individual rights, they also show the genius and forethought our Framers used when planning.

They knew times would call for changes. They knew, as much as they tried, they couldn't think of everything. So they made if possible for the Constitution to be amended. This has occurred eighteen times in our country's history. Yes, there are twenty-seven in all, but Amendments One through Ten were all ratified at once. Together, these first ten Amendments are known as the Bill of Rights.

FOUNDING Father Forum

★ When James Madison first introduced the "amendments" to Congress, he voiced that he felt that the "amendments" be placed in various places within the related articles. For example, the "right to bear arms" amendment would be placed in Article I, Section 9. Others disagreed, saying if the original language of the Constitution were altered, it would "imply that the original language of the Constitution had been defective."

It could also imply the Constitution itself could be altered.

THE BILL OF RIGHTS
Amendments One to Ten

Immediately following the Articles of the Constitution comes a section called the Bill of Rights. The first ten amendments to the Constitution were ratified December 15, 1791. After completing the Constitution, our Framers presented this new document to the rest of America. The Anti-Federalists feared the Constitution would give the government too much power over the people and the states. So they proposed an addition explaining some rights that could not be touched by the government. The Framers of the Constitution did not think that this was necessary, for they had established a government whose powers were numbered; a government that would not be able to take away people's rights. However, after hearing this argument, James Madison wrote twelve additional "amendments," ten of which were adopted, and then became the Bill of Rights.

The Bill of Rights protects many freedoms we take for granted: speech, religion, the right to bear arms, trial by jury, and many more.

LIBERTY Language

The Bill of Rights: This list of Amendments secures the rights of the individual.

TEACHERS' LOUNGE

www.CartoonStock.com

"I don't teach my students about the Bill of Rights any more — it just makes them unruly."

Amendment I

Congress shall make no law respecting an establishment of religion, or prohibiting the free exercise thereof; or abridging the freedom of speech, or of the press; or the right of the people peaceably to assemble, and to petition the Government for a redress of grievances.

The Bottom Line

The First Amendment protects five of your rights: freedom of religion; freedom of speech; freedom of the press; and the rights to assemble and petition the government.

What Were They Thinking?

Our Founding Fathers, especially the Anti-Federalists, wanted to make sure there was a formal document listing the rights of the people to protect them from the government.

Why Should I Care?

The First Amendment prohibits the government from infringing upon your rights. This insures your rights to life, liberty, and the pursuit of happiness. Without this Amendment, you could be jailed for posting on Facebook, or for peaceful gatherings such as the Tea Party.

Today, this clause has been stretched too far and used to prevent government from supporting, or voicing, any religious beliefs—such as the argument to remove the Ten Commandments from the State House.

Breakin' It Down

This amendment breaks down into five clauses. First is the Establishment Clause, which guarantees our freedom of religion. It was incorporated into the first amendment to prevent Congress from establishing an official, nation-wide religion or from supporting one denomination over another. Also, our Founders didn't want Congress to be able to disestablish any existing state churches. They wanted to preserve the people's right of religious expression.

The Free Exercise Clause prevents Congress from interfering with any individual religious beliefs.

SOPA and PIPA

Recently the Freedom of the Press was attacked with SOPA and PIPA, a pair of controversial anti-piracy bills. SOPA is an acronym for the Stop Online Piracy Act, and PIPA stands for Protect IP Act. They were proposed bills that aimed to crack down on copyright infringement, or "pirating," mainly from illegal, overseas sites like The Pirate Bay, where you could type in any current movie or TV show like "Glee" and download full seasons and recent episodes for free. Content providers have battled piracy for years, and while the ideas behind SOPA and PIPA were supported, the wording of the proposed bills would have had far-reaching consequences, including complete Internet censorship. Sites like YouTube would have ceased to exist.

Well hello **Internet** Sorry, but I am here to **take away your freedom**

STOP SOPA & PIPA

STORMGARDENS.CO

Daniel Rojas

The Free Speech Clause protects your freedom to voice your opinion. However, this clause only protects political and peaceful speech, not obscene or violent speech. The Free Press Clause is similar to the Free Speech Clause but relates to the media. The Assembly and Petition Clause protects the rights of the people to assemble and petition the government. Along with voting, petition is a main way for a citizen to voice their opinion to the government.

How Can I Make a Difference?

The government can never take away these rights as long as the Constitution is protected. That is why it is so important for you to raise awareness about it. Pay attention to the news for one day, and see how these rights are violated in other countries, like Syria and Iran.

The Tea Party is a perfect example of peaceful assembly.

What Has It Done For Me Lately?

Every time you go to church, read a web article, or sign a petition to get a vending machine at your school, you are exercising your rights given to you by the First Amendment.

A well regulated Militia, being necessary to the security of a free State, the right of the people to keep and bear Arms, shall not be infringed.

The Bottom Line

The Second Amendment establishes that the militia has the right to secure a state, and you have the right to own a firearm for defense.

What Were They Thinking?

Our Founding Fathers believed the right to bear arms protects the First Amendment, and it was the best guarantee for the United States and its people to remain free.

Our Founders believed that "disarmament was a direct path to slavery."

Why Should I Care?

Amendment II of the United States Constitution is among one of the most cherished rights of American citizens. If the right to bear arms is infringed upon, the chances for invasion and tyrannical control of America greatly increases.

Breakin' It Down

This Amendment gives people the right to bear arms, or own guns, even if not in the military. States also are allowed to organize their own militias.

FOUNDING Father Forum

★ Both Anti-Federalists and Federalists unanimously agreed to protect individuals' rights to bear arms.

Gun Control according to King George III

In England, King George III, wanting to suppress the rebellious spirit of the colonists, stripped the colonists of their right to bear arms through "an aggressive gun control program in 1774-1776." England banned the import of guns and ammunition, confiscated the colonists' personal guns and gunpowder and the central repositories that served as a "holding room" for the town's guns and powder. British soldiers placed Boston under military occupation and went house-to-house confiscating firearms. If the New England towns refused to surrender their firearms, the British navy threatened to bombard and destroy the towns. You can now see why citizens' right to bear arms was so important to our Founders.

Amendment III ★ ★ ★ ★ ★

> *No Soldier shall, in time of peace be quartered in any house, without the consent of the Owner, nor in time of war, but in a manner to be prescribed by law.*

The Bottom Line

The Third Amendment guarantees that you and your family will not be forced to give up your house in times of war or peace to soldiers in the military.

What Were They Thinking?

Our Founding Fathers wanted an amendment that eliminated quartering once and for all.

Why Should I Care?

This clause prevents soldiers, in times of peace on American soil, from barging in and taking over your house! However, during war times, Congress can authorize such quartering usually with compensation to owners.

LIBERTY Language

Quartering: In this sense, refers to the practice of soldiers forcibly moving into peoples' homes usually in times of war.

Quartering Fun (or not-so-fun) Facts:

- Quartering soldiers has been a hot issue since the early 12th century. Actually, it was during the 1066 Norman Conquests that the issue of quartering entered into the lives and households of the people.

- Many ancient charters inadequately addressed the issue of involuntary quartering, naming it unlawful, but the charters were ignored by the despots as quickly as it was written.

- Under the rule of Charles I, parliament refused to fund his many wars, so English soldiers were forced to lodge in private homes and use private buildings as barracks.

- In the mid-18th century, at the close of the French-Indian War, England's parliament passed the Quartering Act, which demanded the colonists "bear all the costs of housing troops." This allowed English soldiers to lodge in private buildings without the consent of the colonists. The English Parliament then passed a second Quartering Act in 1774, allowing English soldiers to lodge in private homes.

You can now see the reason that the colonists were pretty set on abolishing quartering from America's new government.

One of our first complaints, under the former government, was the quartering of troops upon us. This was one of the principal reasons for dissolving the connection with Great Britain. Here we may have troops in time of peace. They may be billeted in any manner — to tyrannize, oppress, and crush us.

PATRICK HENRY

Breakin' It Down

The quartering of soldiers in citizens' houses may now seem like a bizarre thing to worry about or to include in the Bill of Rights, but quartering was a major issue in the years leading up to the Revolutionary War, as American colonists resented the British troops they were forced to put up in their homes.

★ ★ ★ ★ Amendment IV ★ ★ ★ ★ ★

The right of the people to be secure in their persons, houses, papers, and effects, against unreasonable searches and seizures, shall not be violated, and no Warrants shall issue, but upon probable cause, supported by Oath or affirmation, and particularly describing the place to be searched, and the persons or things to be seized.

The Bottom Line

The Fourth Amendment protects you from unreasonable search and seizure and requires probable cause to obtain warrants.

What Were They Thinking?

Our Founding Fathers wanted to insure that America's citizens wouldn't be taken hostage or searched by the government without reason.

Why Should I Care?

Thanks to the Fourth Amendment, an officer cannot seize your belongings, arrest you, or search you or your property without reasonable cause and usually a warrant from a judge.

Breakin' It Down

The Fourth Amendment protects people from undeserved harassment by the police. Police officers have no right to arrest citizens or to search through their personal property without first receiving a warrant, or having justifiable probable cause.

★ ★ ★ ★ ★ Amendment V ★ ★ ★ ★ ★

No person shall be held to answer for a capital, or otherwise infamous crime, unless on a presentment or indictment of a Grand Jury, except in cases arising in the land or naval forces, or in the Militia, when in actual service in time of War or public danger; nor shall any person be subject for the same offence to be twice put in jeopardy of life or limb; nor shall be compelled in any criminal case to be a witness against himself, nor be deprived of life, liberty, or property, without due process of law; nor shall private property be taken for public use, without just compensation.

The Bottom Line

The Fifth Amendment establishes the following:

- Grand Jury: In criminal cases, a grand jury will decide if criminal charges are deserved.

- Double Jeopardy: A person can't be retried for the same crime.

- "Pleading the Fifth:" A person doesn't have to testify against himself in a court of law.

- Due Process: A person can't be convicted without going through the proper procedures, nor keep you on trial after a verdict is reached.

- Improper Seizure: The government can't take your property for public use, without paying a fair price, like taking your home to clear the way for a new road.

What Were They Thinking?

Our Founding Fathers wanted to maintain an uncorrupted judicial system and protect the rights of the accused.

Why Should I Care?

Would you like it if you were declared innocent of a crime, yet the government tried you again? If a government official knocked on your door and claimed your house for government property? The Fifth Amendment prevents these things from happening and more, such as keeping you in jail unfairly for a long time.

Breakin' It Down

In addition to protecting private property from being taken by the government, the Fifth Amendment protects the rights of a person accused of a crime by promising a "grand jury indictment before trial"; protection from testifying against oneself (I plead the Fifth); and guarding against perpetual trials if found "not guilty." A perpetual trial is a trial that continues forever. Take for instance: Betty Sue was charged with stealing a pack of gum from a gas station. The jury ruled the evidence showed otherwise, so Betty Sue was off the hook, being found "not guilty." But the gas station owner might argue and try to prove Betty Sue really did steal the gum, and he could try to get police to continue searching for evidence, keep watching video cameras, or stake out Betty Sue, keeping the trial "perpetually" going even though she had been declared innocent. The Fifth Amendment protects Betty Sue from perpetual trial and prevents her from being hauled into court again on the same charge.

In all criminal prosecutions, the accused shall enjoy the right to a speedy and public trial, by an impartial jury of the State and district wherein the crime shall have been committed, which district shall have been previously ascertained by law, and to be informed of the nature and cause of the accusation; to be confronted with the witnesses against him; to have compulsory process for obtaining witnesses in his favor, and to have the Assistance of Counsel for his defence.

The Bottom Line

The Sixth Amendment protects your many rights in criminal trial.

What Were They Thinking?

The framers of the Constitution were all too familiar with the ways a tyrant deals with imprisoning people: if you had a different opinion than the king in power, you were imprisoned; if you tried to speak up against the king, you were imprisoned; etc. Our Founders wanted to secure that this would never happen in America. Our Founders brilliantly did so with seven elements in the Sixth Amendment to our Constitution.

Why Should I Care?

Without the Sixth Amendment, most, if not all, of your rights in court would not be ensured. Think if you were denied your right to hire an attorney or the right to summon your witnesses.

Breakin' It Down

The Sixth Amendment guarantees the right to a speedy and public trial, an impartial jury, the right to know why you are being arrested, your right to your defendant's cross examination, your right to summon witnesses on your behalf, and your right to hire an attorney. By requiring that an accused citizen have the right to a quick trial, our Founders protected the accused from going through a lengthy period of confinement in jail before their trial.

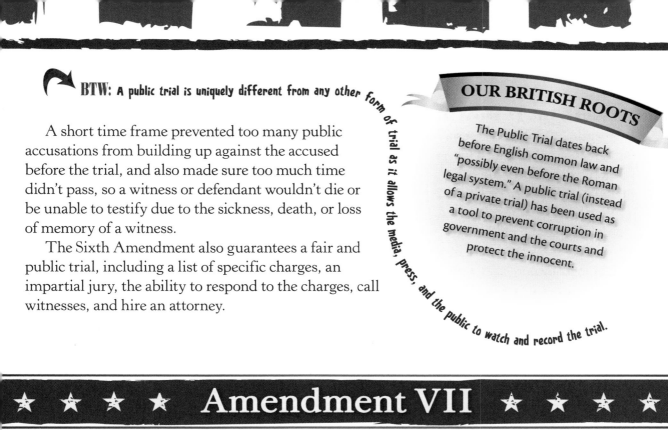

BTW: A public trial is uniquely different from any other form of trial as it allows the media, press, and the public to watch and record the trial.

A short time frame prevented too many public accusations from building up against the accused before the trial, and also made sure too much time didn't pass, so a witness or defendant wouldn't die or be unable to testify due to the sickness, death, or loss of memory of a witness.

The Sixth Amendment also guarantees a fair and public trial, including a list of specific charges, an impartial jury, the ability to respond to the charges, call witnesses, and hire an attorney.

OUR BRITISH ROOTS

The Public Trial dates back before English common law and "possibly even before the Roman legal system." A public trial (instead of a private trial) has been used as a tool to prevent corruption in government and the courts and protect the innocent.

★ ★ ★ ★ Amendment VII ★ ★ ★ ★ ★

In Suits at common law, where the value in controversy shall exceed twenty dollars, the right of trial by jury shall be preserved, and no fact tried by a jury, shall be otherwise re-examined in any Court of the United States, than according to the rules of the common law.

The Bottom Line
The Seventh Amendment guarantees the right to a trial by jury.

What Were They Thinking?
Our Founding Fathers wanted to make sure that the right to trial by jury in ordinary lawsuits between people would be protected, like it was in criminal cases in the Sixth Amendment.

Why Should I Care?
Without this amendment, when you get in a car accident during a vacation in another state and have to sue the other driver for your injuries, your case could be decided by a single person—the judge. However, with this Amendment, you have a chance to argue your case to a jury with, for example, twelve people, who will better understand your case.

Breakin' It Down

Amendment VII promises a fair and just judicial branch with limitations that protect the American people by having a court system which balances the role of judge and jury making neither all-powerful. This amendment states that any common law dispute should have the right to go before a court, having the right to a "trial by jury," meaning that the case will be heard before a jury of usually twelve citizens. Unlike a criminal case in Federal court where the jurors have to be unanimous on their decision.

LIBERTY Language

Civil Case: A legal dispute between two or more parties, like over a stolen car or money owed for rent.

Criminal Case: A case involving a crime of any kind.

Common Law: The Body of English law that the state took over as their own and adapted to their own people.

★ ★ ★ ★ ★ Amendment VIII ★ ★ ★ ★

Excessive bail shall not be required, nor excessive fines imposed, nor cruel and unusual punishments inflicted.

The Bottom Line

Amendment VIII protects against cruel and unusual punishment. The punishment must fit the crime.

What Were They Thinking?

Our Founding Fathers incorporated this amendment into the Bill of Rights to protect you from torture, whipping, branding, ear cropping, drawing, and quartering—all punishments that existed in 1791.

Why Should I Care?

Without Amendment Eight, you could be held in jail by a ridiculously high bail rate, meaning that your parents couldn't afford to pay for your release, and you might have to wait months or years before your case is heard and your innocence proved.

Breakin' It Down

Excessive bail and excessive fines cannot be used to hold a citizen captive in jail, nor can severe punishment be inflicted.

★ ★ ★ ★ Amendment IX ★ ★ ★ ★ ★ ★

The enumeration in the Constitution of certain rights shall not be construed to deny or disparage others retained by the people.

The Bottom Line

Amendment IX said any rights not specified in the Constitution still belong to the people.

What Were They Thinking?

Our Founding Fathers wanted to limit the federal government while protecting the liberties of the people.

Why Should I Care?

Government does not have rights, people have rights. Government has powers. If not for the Ninth Amendment, the government could get away with infringing upon rights that were not specifically listed by the Bill of Rights.

> For example, our government might select two teenagers from each state and force them to participate in a series of games, perhaps to the death, like in *The Hunger Games*, by Suzanne Collins. Or government could practice never-ending mind control, like in *1984*, by George Orwell. Hypothetically, of course.

Breakin' It Down

The first eight amendments to the Bill of Rights declare and protect the freedoms of the people. But Amendments Nine and Ten recognize additional rights out there in the universe not specifically mentioned in the Bill of Rights. Amendment IX states that a person cannot be denied certain rights to freedom by the federal government, just because the Bill of Rights does not enumerate it.

"Don't get all Constitutiony on me, counselor!"

★ ★ ★ ★ ★ Amendment X ★ ★ ★ ★ ★

The powers not delegated to the United States by the Constitution, nor prohibited by it to the States, are reserved to the States respectively, or to the people.

The Bottom Line

Amendment X said any right not given to the national government is the right of the state, as long as the Constitution does not explicitly prohibit the states from that right.

What Were They Thinking?

Our Founding Fathers wanted to ensure that the national government could never overpower the sovereignty and individuality of the states.

Why Should I Care?

This amendment preserves your state's power and sovereignty. Without this amendment, the government could take away many state rights, like the right to hold an annual state fair!

Breakin' It Down

In Amendment Ten, our Founding Fathers clearly voiced their plan for the United States: a group of sovereign states, a government of checks and balances made up of three separate branches that are limited by their enumerated powers, and a people who rule through their representative and of the people of the states to govern themselves.

This ends our Bill of Rights.

★ ★ ★ ★ **Amendment XI** ★ ★ ★ ★ ★ ★

The Judicial power of the United States shall not be construed to extend to any suit in law or equity, commenced or prosecuted against one of the United States by Citizens of another State, or by Citizens or Subjects of any Foreign State.

The Bottom Line

The Eleventh Amendment, ratified on February 7, 1795, in its original intent, prohibits a person from suing a state without its consent.

What Were They Thinking?

Our Founding Fathers set up a system that preserved basic aspects of state sovereignty. One of those was the idea that a state could not be sued without agreeing to it. The 11th Amendment prevents people from suing a state without its consent.

Why Should I Care?

What if you get run over by the local animal control officer? You cannot sue the state unless the state agrees. Many states have agreed to be sued for injuries inflicted by their employees.

Breakin' It Down

Every state ratified this amendment except Pennsylvania and New Jersey. The states were angry because the Supreme Court had allowed a citizen of South Carolina to sue the state of Georgia without its consent for money the state owed to him. The states saw this as an invasion of their rights. So now the federal courts cannot judge a lawsuit against any state without its consent. However, this amendment only applies to states, not cities or counties. Nor does it apply to suits against state officers to stop them from doing something unconstitutional.

What Has It Done For Me Lately?

In the 1993 ruling in *Martin v. Voinovich*, the high court ordered the governor of Ohio to construct housing for handicapped people to comply with the Americans with Disabilities Act.

★ ★ ★ ★ ★ Amendment XII ★ ★ ★ ★ ★

The Electors shall meet in their respective states, and vote by ballot for President and Vice-President, one of whom, at least, shall not be an inhabitant of the same state with themselves; they shall name in their ballots the person voted for as President, and in distinct ballots the person voted for as Vice-President, and they shall make distinct lists of all persons voted for as President, and of all persons voted for as Vice-President and of the number of votes for each, which lists they shall sign and certify, and transmit sealed to the seat of the government of the United States, directed to the President of the Senate;

The President of the Senate shall, in the presence of the Senate and House of Representatives, open all the certificates and the votes shall then be counted;

The person having the greatest Number of votes for President, shall be the President, if such number be a majority of the whole number of Electors appointed; and if no person have such majority, then from the persons having the highest numbers not exceeding three on the list of those voted for as President, the House of Representatives shall choose immediately, by ballot, the President. But in choosing the President, the votes shall be taken by states, the representation from each state having one vote; a quorum for this purpose shall consist of a member or members from two-thirds of the states, and a majority of all the states shall be necessary to a choice. And if the House of Representatives shall not choose a President whenever the right of choice shall devolve upon them, before the fourth day of March next following, then the Vice-President shall act as President, as in the case of the death or other constitutional disability of the President.

The person having the greatest number of votes as Vice-President, shall be the Vice-President, if such number be a majority of the whole number of Electors appointed, and if no person have a majority, then from the two highest numbers on the list, the Senate shall choose the Vice-President; a quorum for the purpose shall consist of two-thirds of the whole number of Senators, and a majority of the whole number shall be necessary to a choice. But no person constitutionally ineligible to the office of President shall be eligible to that of Vice-President of the United States.

The Bottom Line

The Twelfth Amendment, ratified on June 15, 1804, states the president will be the person who receives the majority of the electoral votes. If there isn't a majority, then the Congress will vote from the top three candidates. If there still isn't a majority, then the vice president will be president until the Congress can figure something out. The vice president will be the guy who receives the majority of electoral votes, as long as he meets the constitutional requirements for president.

What Were They Thinking?

The election of 1796 caused a divided administration because the president and VP were from different parties. The heated election of 1800 resulted in a tie in electoral votes between political rivals Jefferson and Aaron Burr. Americans saw the election process and the Electoral College needed a little tweaking.

Why Should I Care?

Without this amendment, our executive branch could be very different, with the possibility of electing a president and vice president from different parties. History would repeat itself. They would be very uncooperative together and nothing would get done!

Breakin' It Down

After the election, John Adams served as president with Thomas Jefferson as VP, both from different political parties. As history revealed, having a president and a vice president from two different parties did not spell "cooperation." By the passing of the Twelfth Amendment, the vice president would now be elected separately.

This amendment also addressed problems within the Electoral College. Prior to Amendment XII, the winner with the most electoral votes became president, and the runner-up became vice president. However, this proved to be quite a mess. In the election of 1800, Federalist John Adams ran against Democratic-Republican Thomas Jefferson, and Aaron Burr as Jefferson's vice presidential running mate. As it turned out, Thomas Jefferson and Aaron Burr got an equal number of votes in the Electoral College from the Democratic-Republic. The reason for the debacle was because the election was not clear-cut. Had one of the nominees received the clear majority of votes, history might have played out differently. Yet Thomas Jefferson and Aaron Burr received the same number of electoral votes, and Burr then decided he wanted to be president instead. Following the rules established in Article II of the Constitution, the election was handed to Congress. After a long delay, Jefferson was elected president, defeating Burr and Adams, marking the first time there had been a change of party in the White House. The three previous elections had elected Washington twice, and then Adams, both f ederalist presidents.

Rock, papers, scissors, two out of three.

I prefer Tic-Tac-Toe.

What Has It Done For Me Lately?

Recently in the election of 2000 between Democratic Candidate Al Gore and Republican Candidate George W. Bush, the Democratic candidate received the majority of popular votes, but the Republican candidate received the majority in the electoral votes. Following the Constitution and this amendment, George W. Bush won the election with the majority of electoral votes, but he did not win the popular vote.

★ ★ ★ ★ Amendment XIII ★ ★ ★ ★ ★ ★

Neither slavery nor involuntary servitude, except as a punishment for crime whereof the party shall have been duly convicted, shall exist within the United States, or any place subject to their jurisdiction.

Congress shall have power to enforce this article by appropriate legislation.

The Bottom Line

The Thirteenth Amendment, ratified on December 6, 1865, abolished slavery in the United States forever.

What Were They Thinking?

Many of our Founding Fathers were opposed to slavery and wanted to stop slavery, but they knew that the Constitution would never have been ratified because the southern states would never have agreed. Thus, they created the amendment process with us so that future generations could abolish slavery in America.

Why Should I Care?

This amendment was a huge step in equality for all people in the United States, just as our Founding Fathers *really* wanted. This amendment ensures that the inalienable rights of life, liberty, and the pursuit of happiness are open to every man in the United States (the 19th Amendment will include women in the picture).

Breakin' It Down

The Thirteenth Amendment to the United States Constitution was ratified on December 6, 1865. In 1776, Americans took the first step on the path of equality by penning the four words "all men are created equal" in the Declaration of Independence. Those four words were revolutionary! But it took one hundred years for slavery to be abolished. Abolishing slavery once and for all, the Thirteenth Amendment, combined with the Fourteenth and Fifteenth Amendments, greatly expanded civil rights for all people.

How Can I Make a Difference?

Write a letter to your representatives about the issue of slavery and trafficking which still exist in other parts of the world. Ask what America can do to help.

What Has It Done For Me Lately?

Even though slavery was abolished more than one hundred years ago, this amendment ensures that slavery will never be allowed in America again. However, slavery and other forms of trafficking still exist in other parts of the world.

In 1780, under the pressure of the anti-slavery Quakers, Pennsylvania passed the "Act for the Gradual Abolition of Slavery." Following the American examples, the English ended slavery in Great Britain with the Slavery Abolition Act in 1833. Fifteen years later, in 1848, France also abolished slavery.

To quote author William J. Bennet in *America: The Last Best Hope*, "One might conclude, that far from being slavery's worst practitioners, westerners led the world to end the practice."

BTW: President Abraham Lincoln proclaimed in his Emancipation Proclamation that all slaves would be free.

1. All persons born or naturalized in the United States, and subject to the jurisdiction thereof, are citizens of the United States and of the State wherein they reside. No State shall make or enforce any law which shall abridge the privileges or immunities of citizens of the United States; nor shall any State deprive any person of life, liberty, or property, without due process of law; nor deny to any person within its jurisdiction the equal protection of the laws.

2. Representatives shall be apportioned among the several States according to their respective numbers, counting the whole number of persons in each State, excluding Indians not taxed. But when the right to vote at any election for the choice of electors for President and Vice-President of the United States, Representatives in Congress, the Executive and Judicial officers of a State, or the members of the Legislature thereof, is denied to any of the male inhabitants of such State, being twenty-one years of age, and citizens of the United States, or in any way abridged, except for participation in rebellion, or other crime, the basis of representation therein shall be reduced in the proportion which the number of such male citizens shall bear to the whole number of male citizens twenty-one years of age in such State.

3. No person shall be a Senator or Representative in Congress, or elector of President and Vice-President, or hold any office, civil or military, under the United States, or under any State, who, having previously taken an oath, as a member of Congress, or as an officer of the United States, or as a member of any State legislature, or as an executive or judicial officer of any State, to support the Constitution of the United States, shall have engaged in insurrection or rebellion against the same, or given aid or comfort to the enemies thereof. But Congress may by a vote of two-thirds of each House, remove such disability.

4. The validity of the public debt of the United States, authorized by law, including debts incurred for payment of pensions and bounties for services in suppressing insurrection or rebellion, shall not be questioned. But neither the United States nor any State shall assume or pay any debt or obligation incurred in aid of insurrection or rebellion against the United States, or any claim for the loss or emancipation of any slave; but all such debts, obligations and claims shall be held illegal and void.

5. The Congress shall have power to enforce, by appropriate legislation, the provisions of this article.

The Bottom Line

The Fourteenth Amendment, ratified on July 9, 1868, establishes four things. First, all people born in the U.S. are legally citizens and receive all benefits of citizenship. Second, the three-fifth's clause was repealed. Third, former Confederate leaders (or anyone who takes part in any form of rebellion against the U.S.) can't vote or hold office (unless two-thirds of Congress votes okay). Fourth, no Confederate states, or Americans who aided the Confederate Army, will get any compensation from the federal government for Civil War debts or "loss of property."

What Were They Thinking?

The first ten amendments prevent *Congress* from infringing on our rights, but after the Civil War it was recognized that *states* would have to follow the same rules on how they treat their citizens.

Why Should I Care?

The first clause of this amendment is important to every American citizen, making anyone born in the U.S. an automatic U.S. citizen. Otherwise, in addition to tons of vaccines and examinations right after birth, we would also have to pass a citizenship test!

Breakin' It Down

The first section of the amendment includes four crucial elements. First, anyone born on American soil is guaranteed full American citizenship. Second, no state can strip any of its residents of the full privileges of American citizenship. Third, all citizens are guaranteed "due process of law," which means that states cannot pass arbitrary or unfair laws. Fourth, all citizens are guaranteed "equal protection of the laws," which means that states cannot discriminate against particular groups of citizens.

★ ★ ★ ★ Amendment XV ★ ★ ★ ★ ★

The right of citizens of the United States to vote shall not be denied or abridged by the United States or by any State on account of race, color, or previous condition of servitude.

The Congress shall have power to enforce this article by appropriate legislation.

The Bottom Line

The Fifteenth Amendment, ratified on February 3, 1870, says no one can be denied their right to vote on the basis of race, color, or previous servitude.

What Were They Thinking?

The Founders knew the Constitution wasn't perfect and that times would change. Back then, only property owners could vote, but our Founders expected voting rights to change by later amendments.

Why Should I Care?

This amendment was a first step toward the promises guaranteed in the Declaration of Independence and Constitution.

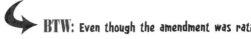

BTW: Even though the amendment was ratified in 1870, the  amendment was not put into practice until the passage of the Voting Rights Act in 1965.

Breakin' It Down

Amendment Fifteen gave male citizens the right to vote regardless of race. Congress passed this amendment on February 26, 1869, but it took almost a year before it was ratified by the states. Though Amendment Fifteen completed the three-part series of civil rights amendments, in practice, it didn't work very well.

How Can I Make a Difference?

Exercise your right to vote. Participate in mock elections at your school. Never underestimate the importance of your vote—it forms the basis of our democracy!

What Has It Done For Me Lately?

This amendment comes into play every election cycle! Go with your parents when they vote.

It would take fifty more years for women across America to be given the right to vote, but the Fifteenth Amendment was a large leap toward the equality of rights. Remember, your vote is your voice!

Make sure your parents vote!

BTW: Before the Voting Rights Act of 1965, states prohibited citizens from voting in many ways, such as literacy tests, which prohibited citizens from voting if they couldn't read and write.

Amendment XVI

The Congress shall have power to lay and collect taxes on incomes, from whatever source derived, without apportionment among the several States, and without regard to any census or enumeration.

The Bottom Line

The Sixteenth Amendment, ratified on February 3, 1913, allowes Congress to place a tax on the money we receive as income in order to raise money for the U.S. government.

What Were They Thinking?

Direct taxes were generally unpopular and rarely used by the federal government. Our Founding Fathers feared that taxes would turn the North and South against each other because the North, having more people, would pay more and the South, with less people would pay less.

And Americans have been complaining ever since!

Why Should I Care?

When our parents receive their paychecks, a percentage of that amount is taken out and given to the government. The same thing will occur when we receive our paychecks. It's important to know which amendment gives government the right to take some of our hard-earned money.

Can you think of alternative ways for the government to raise money? Perhaps a bake sale?

Breakin' It Down

Income taxes were not mentioned until the Civil War, when Congress needed a way to increase revenue. In 1861, the Congress passed the temporary Revenue Act, which "levied a flat tax of 3% on annual income above $800 (or $20,000 in today's dollars)." However, this was only a temporary income tax, expiring in 1893. Shortly afterwards, Congress attempted to distribute a federal tax "on income derived from real estate." The Supreme Court declared this law unconstitutional. After the turn of the century, President William Taft requested, through a formal message, that Congress adopt an income tax amendment. Congress, who was already searching for more profitable sources of income, accepted the idea with open arms.

How Can I Make a Difference?

Go to IRS.gov or ask your parents to learn more about how taxes are calculated based on income. See how taxes are calculated for people with part-time jobs.

1. The Senate of the United States shall be composed of two Senators from each State, elected by the people thereof, for six years; and each Senator shall have one vote. The electors in each State shall have the qualifications requisite for electors of the most numerous branch of the State legislatures.

2. When vacancies happen in the representation of any State in the Senate, the executive authority of such State shall issue writs of election to fill such vacancies: Provided, That the legislature of any State may empower the executive thereof to make temporary appointments until the people fill the vacancies by election as the legislature may direct.

3. This amendment shall not be so construed as to affect the election or term of any Senator chosen before it becomes valid as part of the Constitution.

The Bottom Line

The Seventeenth Amendment, ratified on April 8, 1913, says senators would be elected by the people instead of state legislatures.

What Were They Thinking?

Our Founding Fathers assigned the branches of government, the election processes, and the enumerated powers in a way they thought would be most productive. However, people at the turn of the twentieth century thought more participation by voters was needed. Some opponents of this amendment argue that it has weakened the power of the states.

Why Should I Care?

Corruption by government officials is very real. Our Framers knew this and provided checks and balances to help, but they also believed that the majority would ultimately prevail and prevent corrupt officials from taking over. You are part of the majority. Be on the lookout for dishonesty in our elected officials.

Breakin' It Down

The Seventeenth Amendment was a result of a long erosion of the process of electing senators to the federal Congress. The election process worked for many years, but at the end of the 19th century, some states adopted preference elections, where the people could vote for their preferred candidate. The state legislatures would then elect the winner of that preference election. This method effectively allowed the people to elect senators instead of the state legislatures. Over time, more and more favored direct popular election, resulting in the 17th Amendment.

How Can I Make a Difference?
Become aware of proposed ideas for new amendments and study them to see if they are constitutional.

What Has It Done For Me Lately?
Not only do the people elect members of the Senate, thanks to the Internet, you can stream live Senate floor proceedings at Senate.gov, as well as download previous proceedings, starting with the 2nd session of the 112th Congress.

★ ★ ★ ★ Amendment XVIII ★ ★ ★ ★ ★ ★

1. After one year from the ratification of this article the manufacture, sale, or transportation of intoxicating liquors within, the importation thereof into, or the exportation thereof from the United States and all territory subject to the jurisdiction thereof for beverage purposes is hereby prohibited.

2. The Congress and the several States shall have concurrent power to enforce this article by appropriate legislation.

3. This article shall be inoperative unless it shall have been ratified as an amendment to the Constitution by the legislatures of the several States, as provided in the Constitution, within seven years from the date of the submission hereof to the States by the Congress.

The Bottom Line
The Eighteenth Amendment, ratified on December 18, 1917, outlawed liquor.

What Were They Thinking?
Our Founding Fathers rarely in the Constitution ever prohibited the abilities and freedoms of the people. This amendment is a good example of what happens when the government tries to go too far in prohibiting the people's rights.

➤ **BTW:** Amendment Eighteen is the only amendment that restricted citizens' rights, and the only one repealed by a later amendment.

Why Should I Care?

Even though this amendment was repealed, it's still a good example of the power of the government. If the government and the states can ratify an amendment prohibiting the consumption of alcohol, they could pass all kinds of crazy amendments—they could prohibit drinking soda! For this reason we have to pay attention to who is elected into our national government.

The eighteenth amendment is a good example of trial and error.

Breakin' It Down

This amendment banned liquor in the United States. The evils of alcohol had been preached since early colonial days, and Massachusetts banned "strong liquor" in 1657. But the temperance, anti-alcohol, movement gained momentum after the Civil War with the rise of the Prohibition Party and the Women's Christian Temperance Union. The prohibition lobby became so great during World War I that Congress proposed this amendment, and it was ratified by the states. However, Connecticut and Rhode Island never ratified it! As a direct result of prohibition, illegal, or bootleg, liquor became available, and organized crime families and outlaws thrived. Despite good intentions, Congress and the states completely changed their view on prohibition and repealed this amendment less than twenty years later.

★ ★ ★ ★ ★ Amendment XIX ★ ★ ★ ★ ★

The right of citizens of the United States to vote shall not be denied or abridged by the United States or by any State on account of sex.

Congress shall have power to enforce this article by appropriate legislation.

The Bottom Line

The Nineteenth Amendment, ratified on August 18, 1920, guaranteed women's right to vote.

What Were They Thinking?

This amendment was the direct result of the Women's Suffrage movement (the movement for equality of women's rights) across America at this time. American women were becoming more involved and independent, and Washington had no choice but to listen.

Women's Suffragette Movement

- According to the *New York Times*, in the first election in which women were free to vote – the Presidential election of 1920 – some districts accumulated more female voters than male votes!

- Women all over the United States fought for their unalienable rights for seventy-two years. The main reason women wanted their voting rights to be free from infringement, was because they wanted their voice to be heard on issues such as child labor laws and universal education.

- Before the 19th Amendment was adopted, 15 of 48 states already allowed women full voting rights, another 13 allowed voting for president, and all but seven states allowed women to vote in some elections (federal, state, local).

- Since 1920, when women received their right to vote, a total of 276 women have served in the legislative branch of our federal government: 237 congresswomen and 39 senators. Before women could even vote, Belva Lockwood, in 1884 and 1888, was the first woman to ever run for the presidency, actually receiving the electoral votes from the state of Indiana and receiving more than one thousand popular votes from New York and Illinois! Sadly these votes were overturned.

Why Should I Care?

Calling all women! This amendment is the only thing that gives you the ability to vote. Think if this amendment had never been ratified and how different our elections would be in America!

Breakin' It Down

Not even two months after the ratification of this amendment, women from all walks of life joined the rest of the country in walking into polling booths and dropping their ballot into that voting box. You can simply imagine the faces of the women as they slipped their ballot into the voting box for the first time, realizing that their voice was finally being heard.

★ ★ ★ ★ Amendment XX ★ ★ ★ ★ ★ ★

1. The terms of the President and Vice President shall end at noon on the 20th day of January, and the terms of Senators and Representatives at noon on the 3d day of January, of the years in which such terms would have ended if this article had not been ratified; and the terms of their successors shall then begin.

2. The Congress shall assemble at least once in every year, and such meeting shall begin at noon on the 3d day of January, unless they shall by law appoint a different day.

3. If, at the time fixed for the beginning of the term of the President, the President elect shall have died, the Vice President elect shall become President. If a President shall not have been chosen before the time fixed for the beginning of his term, or if the President elect shall have failed to qualify, then the Vice President elect shall act as President until a President shall have qualified; and the Congress may by law provide for the case wherein neither a President elect nor a Vice President elect shall have qualified, declaring who shall then act as President, or the manner in which one who is to act shall be selected, and such person shall act accordingly until a President or Vice President shall have qualified.

4. The Congress may by law provide for the case of the death of any of the persons from whom the House of Representatives may choose a President whenever the right of choice shall have devolved upon them, and for the case of the death of any of the persons from whom the Senate may choose a Vice President whenever the right of choice shall have devolved upon them.

5. Sections 1 and 2 shall take effect on the 15th day of October following the ratification of this article.

6. This article shall be inoperative unless it shall have been ratified as an amendment to the Constitution by the legislatures of three-fourths of the several States within seven years from the date of its submission.

The Bottom Line
The Twentieth Amendment, ratified on January 23, 1933, attempted to do away with "lame-duck" sessions of Congress.

What Were They Thinking?
Our Founding Fathers were always intent on keeping Congress accountable to the people. However, slow communication and transportation made it neccessary to allow enough time between the election and the date for taking office. In their day it took a long time for newly elected officials to get to the capital. This amendment allows the newly elected representatives to take office more quickly.

Why Should I Care?

Representatives voted out of office—lame-duck representatives—still had four more months to pass legislation before the next Congress took over. After this amendment, this time has been cut in half. However, there is still some risk that those leaving office could feasibly pass questionable legislation—since they were no longer responsible to the people.

Breakin' It Down

Prior to the Twentieth Amendment, the terms of the newly elected president, vice president, senators, and representatives did not begin until March. This resulted in a four-month lag time between when the election ended and when the newly elected officials took office. This time period was the lame-duck session. The Twentieth Amendment specifies when the terms of the president and vice president shall end—the 20th day of January at noon. Congressional terms end a couple weeks earlier, January 3, also at noon. This amendment also addresses what happens if the president elect has died or is ill when he is due to take office (the VP steps in), and if something really strange occurs and neither the president elect nor the vice president elect is available to take office (Congress appoints temporary stand-ins).

★ ★ ★ ★ Amendment XXI ★ ★ ★ ★ ★

1. The eighteenth article of amendment to the Constitution of the United States is hereby repealed.

2. The transportation or importation into any State, Territory, or possession of the United States for delivery or use therein of intoxicating liquors, in violation of the laws thereof, is hereby prohibited.

3. This article shall be inoperative unless it shall have been ratified as an amendment to the Constitution by conventions in the several States, as provided in the Constitution, within seven years from the date of the submission hereof to the States by the Congress.

The Bottom Line

The Twenty-First Amendment, ratified on December 5, 1933, lifted the ban on the sale and consumption of alcoholic beverages.

What Were They Thinking?

The Twenty-First Amendment gave the states absolute control over the sales of liquor. It was a compromise with the temperance movement.

Why Should I Care?

Every time you walk into a restaurant and see a busy bar, you are seeing the works of the Twenty-First Amendment. Without this amendment, alcoholic beverages would be against the law.

BTW: South Carolina was the sole state that rejected the 21st Amendment.

Amendment Twenty-One to the United States Constitution repealed the Eighteenth Amendment to the Constitution that prohibited the consumption and sale of alcohol. Amendment Twenty-One is the only amendment that repeals a previous amendment to the Constitution.

Breakin' It Down

The attempts to outlaw alcoholic beverages were failing. Instead of prohibiting alcohol, it sparked a string of smugglers who would sneak alcohol across state lines. This amendment was ratified sixteen years after the Eighteenth Amendment. However, the only way to repeal prohibition was by passing another amendment that declared the lift of the ban on alcohol. This amendment was the only one to be approved by a constitutional convention in the state instead of going through the state legislature. This was because the Eighteenth Amendment had passed as a result of great political pressure on state legislatures by the temperance movement (think lobbyists). The supporters of the Twenty-First Amendment feared it would lose in the state legislatures.

★ ★ ★ ★ ★ Amendment XXII ★ ★ ★ ★ ★

1. No person shall be elected to the office of the President more than twice, and no person who has held the office of President, or acted as President, for more than two years of a term to which some other person was elected President shall be elected to the office of the President more than once. But this Article shall not apply to any person holding the office of President, when this Article was proposed by the Congress, and shall not prevent any person who may be holding the office of President, or acting as President, during the term within which this Article becomes operative from holding the office of President or acting as President during the remainder of such term.

2. This article shall be inoperative unless it shall have been ratified as an amendment to the Constitution by the legislatures of three-fourths of the several States within seven years from the date of its submission to the States by the Congress.

The Bottom Line

The Twenty-Second Amendment, ratified on February 27, 1951, limited the president to two terms, or eight years, in office.

What Were They Thinking?

Our Founding Fathers would disagree with this amendment. They believed that if a leader was popular enough to be elected for multiple terms, then allow the voters to elect him as many times as they choose. Our Founders carefully set up the framework of our country so that if a president *is* elected multiple times, frequent elections would keep the president in check.

Why Should I Care?

This amendment forbids any person from running for president more than twice and prohibits any person from persuading the American people to elect him over and over again. This eliminates the possibility of a dictatorship.

Breakin it Down

This amendment prohibits any president from seeking more than two terms in office, or eight years. However, if a vice president has to take over the office of the presidency, then he can either seek one or two terms depending on how much of the prior president's term he is serving. The most a vice president can ever serve is ten years. Take for example the situation of JFK and Vice President Lyndon B. Johnson. Vice President

FOUNDING Father Forum

★ For years prior to this amendment, presidents either followed the example of President George Washington and did not seek a third term, or their career as president ended through the election process.

Johnson assumed the role of presidency after JFK's assassination. He then ran for president in 1964. He planned to do so again in 1968 but then chose to opt out. If Kennedy had been assassinated a year earlier, President Johnson would not have been able to run for reelection in 1968.

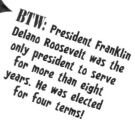

BTW: President Franklin Delano Roosevelt was the only president to serve for more than eight years. He was elected for four terms!

How Can I Make a Difference?
Knowledge is power! Research Franklin Delano Roosevelt and his presidency. What did he do to get elected so many times? What did he do while he was in office?

★ ★ ★ ★ ★ Amendment XXIII ★ ★ ★ ★ ★

1. The District constituting the seat of government of the United States shall appoint in such manner as the Congress may direct: A number of electors of President and Vice President equal to the whole number of Senators and Representatives in Congress to which the District would be entitled if it were a state, but in no event more than the least populous state; they shall be in addition to those appointed by the states, but they shall be considered, for the purposes of the election of President and Vice President, to be electors appointed by a state; and they shall meet in the District and perform such duties as provided by the twelfth article of amendment.

2. The Congress shall have power to enforce this article by appropriate legislation.

The Bottom Line
The Twenty-Third Amendment, ratified on March 29, 1961, grants residents of Washington D.C. the authority to vote in presidential elections and choose electors for the Electoral College.

What Were They Thinking?
Our Founding Fathers purposefully designed the capital so that it would not be a state or part of any state in the Union. Rather, they intended that the District of Columbia would solely serve as the capital of the United States and as the home of the Congress and the president.

Why Should I Care?
Having our capital separate from any state guarantees that it will never be seceded from the Union.

Breakin' It Down

The residents of D.C. originally did not enjoy privileges such as sending members to Congress, voting for president, or electing city councils. With the passing of the 23rd Amendment, however, residents of our nation's capital were granted one of the privileges of a United States citizen: voting for president. Article I, Section 8, Clause 17 allows Congress to preside over the District and "exercise exclusive legislation in all cases whatsoever." Thanks to Amendment 23, the residents of the District of Columbia could vote in presidential elections and be represented in the Electoral College. However, this amendment does not make the District of Columbia a state and does not grant the district any privileges of a state, except the right to be represented in the Electoral College.

BTW: D.C. is given the same number of electors of the least populous state, Wyoming, which had just three electors in 2010.

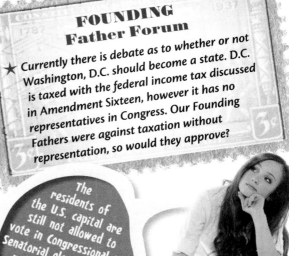

FOUNDING Father Forum

★ Currently there is debate as to whether or not Washington, D.C. should become a state. D.C. is taxed with the federal income tax discussed in Amendment Sixteen, however it has no representatives in Congress. Our Founding Fathers were against taxation without representation, so would they approve?

The residents of the U.S. capital are still not allowed to vote in Congressional and Senatorial elections. It was not until 1970 that D.C. received its one and only non-voting representative.

★ ★ ★ ★ Amendment XXIV ★ ★ ★ ★ ★ ★

1. The right of citizens of the United States to vote in any primary or other election for President or Vice President, for electors for President or Vice President, or for Senator or Representative in Congress, shall not be denied or abridged by the United States or any state by reason of failure to pay any poll tax or other tax.

2. The Congress shall have power to enforce this article by appropriate legislation.

BTW: North Carolina did not ratify this amendment until May 3 of 1989, twenty-seven years after the ratification of the amendment to the Constitution.

The Bottom Line

The Twenty-Fourth Amendment, ratified on January 23, 1964, abolished the poll tax, a tax you had to pay before you could cast your vote.

What Were They Thinking?

Our Founding Fathers believed that voting was a privilege that should be restricted to those who have a lot at stake in the community, so many states had requirements for property ownership and tax requirements, or tests like the literacy test. Over the years, the property qualifications and tax qualifications were gradually eliminated. The poll tax, however, remained until this amendment.

Why Should I Care?

If not for this amendment, you would be forced to pay a tax before you placed your vote during an election. This not only would be a huge hassle, but it would also inhibit some people from voting.

Breakin' It Down

Under the poll tax a citizen could only vote if he or she paid the "poll tax" that was collected from them before they cast their ballot. Also, if the citizen had not paid the fee in past elections, they would have to pay the total sum of all their unpaid poll taxes before they could proceed to vote. The poll tax was a revenue source for state and federal governments. A poll tax was sometimes a large fee, or sometimes, like in Virginia, as little as $1.50 per person (or $10.00 in today's money).

Poll Tax Filibuster

The House of Representatives composed legislation that abolished the poll tax, but it was not passed in the Senate, due to a Southern-led Senate filibuster that blocked the amendment. In 1944, the House tried once more to pass legislation that would abolish the poll tax, however, the House ran into a rather large problem. In Article I, the Constitution places voting qualification in the hands of the states, and with the 15th and 19th Amendments already under their belt, some people argued that any additional legislation limiting a state's power had to be a constitutional amendment.

The push for the abolition of the poll tax began in the 1930s with President FDR, who sided with the Republican Party (not his base party, the Democrats), in their movement to rid the whole nation of the poll tax.

★ ★ ★ ★ ★ Amendment XXV ★ ★ ★ ★ ★

1. In case of the removal of the President from office or of his death or resignation, the Vice President shall become President.

2. Whenever there is a vacancy in the office of the Vice President, the President shall nominate a Vice President who shall take office upon confirmation by a majority vote of both Houses of Congress.

3. Whenever the President transmits to the President pro tempore of the Senate and the Speaker of the House of Representatives his written declaration that he is unable to discharge the powers and duties of his office, and until he transmits to them a written declaration to the contrary, such powers and duties shall be discharged by the Vice President as Acting President.

4. Whenever the Vice President and a majority of either the principal officers of the executive departments or of such other body as Congress may by law provide, transmit to the President pro tempore of the Senate and the Speaker of the House of Representatives their written declaration that the President is unable to discharge the powers and duties of his office, the Vice President shall immediately assume the powers and duties of the office as Acting President.

Thereafter, when the President transmits to the President pro tempore of the Senate and the Speaker of the House of Representatives his written declaration that no inability exists, he shall resume the powers and duties of his office unless the Vice President and a majority of either the principal officers of the executive department or of such other body as Congress may by law provide, transmit within four days to the President pro tempore of the Senate and the Speaker of the House of Representatives their written declaration that the President is unable to discharge the powers and duties of his office. Thereupon Congress shall decide the issue, assembling within forty eight hours for that purpose if not in session. If the Congress, within twenty one days after receipt of the latter written declaration, or, if Congress is not in session, within twenty one days after Congress is required to assemble, determines by two thirds vote of both Houses that the President is unable to discharge the powers and duties of his office, the Vice President shall continue to discharge the same as Acting President; otherwise, the President shall resume the powers and duties of his office.

BTW: Amendments get longer through the years.

The Bottom Line
The Twenty-Fifth Amendment, ratified on February 10, 1967, was the back-up plan for the presidency.

BTW: In the course of American history, seven vice presidents have passed away, two vice presidents have resigned, and nine had to assume the presidency.

What Were They Thinking?

With the passing of the Twenty-Fifth Amendment, regardless of our Founding Fathers' true intent, the issue of the vice president's role was set into stone.

Why Should I Care?

We know that it is always good to have a clear and workable "Plan B" if something goes awry. Our Founding Fathers and the crafters of this amendment thought with the passage of this amendment, we had a backup plan if ever a president was killed or something.

Amendment 25 to the Rescue!

Times the 25th Amendment could have came into play...

• President Garfield was in a coma for eighty days before he passed away due to assassination.

• Woodrow Wilson had a debilitating stroke approximately a year-and-a half before his term was completed.

• President Eisenhower suffered from a heart attack and a stroke while president.

Breakin' It Down

This amendment established what would happen if the president died while in office or became incapable of performing his duties. First, in case of death, the VP would take over. If there is no current VP, Congress would appoint a new VP, who could act for the president temporarily if the president knows he will, per se, be in surgery for a few days. Finally, if the president is incapacitated and won't admit it, the VP, with the consent of the Congress, can remove him from office.

What Has It Done For Me Lately?

If the president ever has to have a medical surgery or operation, this amendment calls for the vice president to take the office, but only for the time the president is unable to serve. When President Bush and President Reagan had colonoscopies, their vice presidents took over during the operation.

★ ★ ★ ★ ★ Amendment XXVI ★ ★ ★ ★ ★

1. The right of citizens of the United States, who are 18 years of age or older, to vote, shall not be denied or abridged by the United States or any state on account of age.

2. The Congress shall have the power to enforce this article by appropriate legislation.

The Bottom Line

The Twenty-Sixth Amendment, ratified on July 1, 1971, lowered the voting age from age twenty-one to eighteen.

What Were They Thinking?

This amendment was brought to the forefront of the conversation because in the late 1900s, young citizens who were already working and feeding families wanted to voice their opinions in the polling booths. And since the same young men could be drafted into the army during war, young adults felt they should be able to vote.

Why Should I Care?

Since this amendment lowers the voting age, our voices will be heard in our government at an earlier point in our lives. This is why it is so important for us to vote and understand our Constitution.

This is very important to us as America's youth

Breakin' It Down

This amendment further limits the power of the government to restrict the right to vote. As the 15th Amendment did with race and the 19th Amendment did with women's voting rights, with this amendment, eighteen-year-olds are now able to vote.

★ ★ ★ ★ Amendment XXVII ★ ★ ★ ★ ★

> *No law varying the compensation for the services of the Senators and Representatives shall take effect until an election of Representatives shall have intervened.*

The Bottom Line

The Twenty-Seventh Amendment, the last amendment, ratified on May 7, 1992, issued that Congress cannot raise their own pay, only the pay of future representatives.

Convention Chat

The first members of Congress were paid per diem, or per day. The first annual salary received by congressional members in 1815 was $1,500. More than 150 years later, in 1968, congressional salaries rose to the rate of $30,000 per year. In 2009, congressional pay rates stood at $174,000 per year!

What Were They Thinking?

We want our representatives to earn enough money so not only the wealthiest are able to be in Congress, but we don't want them draining our country of money either. This Amendment ensures that our representatives must face the voters before they can raise their pay.

Why Should I Care?

Having this Amendment makes members of Congress more cautious because they now have to face the people before they can benefit from their raises.

Breakin' It Down

The paycheck given to our representatives in Washington is left up to Congress itself, according to Article I, Section 6 of the United States Constitution. This, in a way, is like a boss telling his employees they can choose their salaries. Amendment 27 prohibits an increase in Congressional pay from going into effect until after the next election.

How Can I Make a Difference?

Gregory Watson (in box) is a great example of how *you* can make a difference. If there is something that you have learned either from this book or in the news, write to your representative about the issue. To find your representative, go to www.house.gov and www.senate.gov.

BTW: This Amendment was part of the original twelve amendments proposed by James Madison! This Amendment had lain dormant for around 215 years.

How one young person made a difference

Gregory Watson and Amendment 27

The ratification of this amendment was due to the actions of a young citizen by the name of Gregory Watson, a student at the University of Texas at the time. It began when he wrote a term paper arguing for ratification of this amendment. He then embarked on a one-man campaign for the amendment's ratification by writing letters to several state legislatures of different states across the nation. Shortly thereafter, approximately a year after Watson's college term paper, Maine and Colorado ratified the amendment. Then more and more states followed. Today only Massachusetts, Pennsylvania and New York have yet to ratify the amendment!

Who Knows! You could spark a Constitutional Convention or a whole new amendment.

Pop Quiz!
Test your Constitution Knowledge

1. Name five powers given to the federal government in the Constitution that were not granted under the Articles of Confederation.

2. Why are the checks and balances so important? Which articles address the checks and balances?

3. Which article addresses the amendment process? What are the two ways that an amendment can be done?

4. Which branch of government has the power to declare war? Which branch has the power to fund the war? Why?

5. Does the president have the sole power to negotiate and sign a treaty?

6. What is the impeachment process for the president of the United States, and how are the three branches of government intertwined in this process?

7. What was the compromise at the Constitutional Convention in 1787 that resulted in the bicameral congress?

8. How many times is the word "treason" used in the U.S. Constitution? Why were the Framers so concerned about it? Define the different types of treason today.

9. Did James Madison and Alexander Hamilton think the Bill of Rights was necessary? Why or why not?

10. Who constitutes the modern day militia, and under what condition can they spend nights in your home?

11. When police are searching a perpetrator of a crime's house for evidence of a crime, which amendment prevents them from also searching your house if you live on the same block?

12. Why are the 9th and 10th Amendments more important today than when they were ratified?

13. Could the Bill of Rights survive without Articles 1, 2, and 3? Why or why not?

Pop Quiz! Here is the key to the portrait on page 12. How did you do?

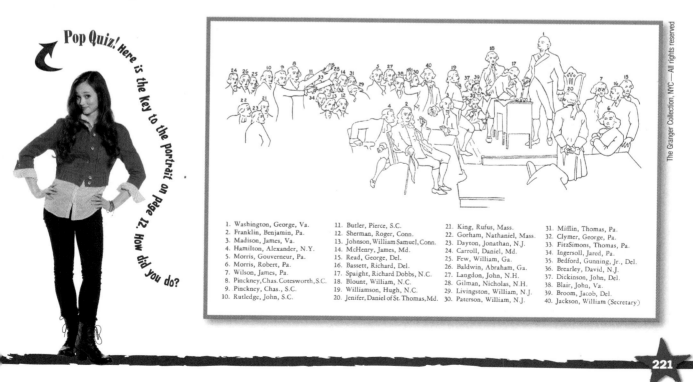

1. Washington, George, Va.
2. Franklin, Benjamin, Pa.
3. Madison, James, Va.
4. Hamilton, Alexander, N.Y.
5. Morris, Gouverneur, Pa.
6. Morris, Robert, Pa.
7. Wilson, James, Pa.
8. Pinckney, Chas. Cotesworth, S.C.
9. Pinckney, Chas., S.C.
10. Rutledge, John, S.C.
11. Butler, Pierce, S.C.
12. Sherman, Roger, Conn.
13. Johnson, William Samuel, Conn.
14. McHenry, James, Md.
15. Read, George, Del.
16. Bassett, Richard, Del.
17. Spaight, Richard Dobbs, N.C.
18. Blount, William, N.C.
19. Williamson, Hugh, N.C.
20. Jenifer, Daniel of St. Thomas, Md.
21. King, Rufus, Mass.
22. Gorham, Nathaniel, Mass.
23. Dayton, Jonathan, N.J.
24. Carroll, Daniel, Md.
25. Few, William, Ga.
26. Baldwin, Abraham, Ga.
27. Langdon, John, N.H.
28. Gilman, Nicholas, N.H.
29. Livingston, William, N.J.
30. Paterson, William, N.J.
31. Mifflin, Thomas, Pa.
32. Clymer, George, Pa.
33. FitzSimons, Thomas, Pa.
34. Ingersoll, Jared, Pa.
35. Bedford, Gunning, Jr., Del.
36. Brearley, David, N.J.
37. Dickinson, John, Del.
38. Blair, John, Va.
39. Broom, Jacob, Del.
40. Jackson, William (Secretary)

Bibliography

Essayists for Constituting America

"Analyzing the Constitution in 90 Days," *Constituting America*. All last accessed April 27, 2012.

Addington, David. "Article I, Section 3, Clause 4-5 of the United States Constitution," *Analyzing the Constitution in 90 Days*. Constituting America, March 3, 2011, http://www.constitutingamerica.org/blog/?p=740

Aden, Steven H. "Article I, Section 6, Clause 2 of the United States Constitution," March 14, 2011, http://www.constitutingamerica.org/blog/?p=871

___. "Amendment IX of the United States Constitution," May 31, 2011, http://www.constitutingamerica.org/blog/?p=1482

Allen, W.B., PhD. "Article I, Section 2, Clause 3 of the United States Constitution," February 24, 2011, http://www.constitutingamerica.org/blog/?p=719

___. Article I, Section 9, Clause 1 of the United States Constitution," April 4, 2011, http://www.constitutingamerica.org/blog/?p=1017

Baker, John S. Jr., PhD. "Article I, Section 8, Clause 1 of the United States Constitution," March 18, 2011, http://www.constitutingamerica.org/blog/?p=916

___. "Article I, Section 8, Clause 3 of the United States Constitution," March 22, 2011, http://www.constitutingamerica.org/blog/?p=933

___. "Amendment XVII of the United States Constitution," June 10, 2011, http://www.constitutingamerica.org/blog/?p=1550

Baskin, Andrew. "Article II, Section 2, Clause 1 of the United States Constitution," April 26, 2011, http://www.constitutingamerica.org/blog/?p=1267

Best, James D. "Article II, Section 1, Clause 5 of the United States Constitution," April 20, 2011, http://www.constitutingamerica.org/blog/?p=1209

Bobb, David J. PhD. "The Preamble to the United States Constitution," February 21, 2011, http://www.constitutingamerica.org/blog/?p=703

Butterfield, Justin. "Article I, Section 10, Clause 2 of the United States Constitution," April 12, 2011, http://www.constitutingamerica.org/blog/?p=1172

Chapman-Smith, Robert. "Amendment III of the United States Constitution," May 23, 2011, http://www.constitutingamerica.org/blog/?p=1433

Cooper, Horace. "Article I, Section 2, Clause 1-2 of the United States Constitution," February 23, 2011, http://www.constitutingamerica.org/blog/?p=714

___. "Article I, Section 8, Clause 4 of the United States Constitution," March 23, 2011, http://www.constitutingamerica.org/blog/?p=944

___. "Article I, Section 8, Clause 10-13 of the United States Constitution," March 29, 2011, http://www.constitutingamerica.org/blog/?p=971

___. "Article III, Section 3, Clause 1-2 of the United States Constitution," May 9, 2011, http://www.constitutingamerica.org/blog/?p=1335

___. "Amendment XVI of the United States Constitution," June 9, 2011, http://www.constitutingamerica.org/blog/?p=1542

___. "Amendment XXIII of the United States Constitution," June 20, 2011, http://www.constitutingamerica.org/blog/?p=1604

Crossed, Carol. "Amendment XIX of the United States Constitution," June 14, 2011, http://www.constitutingamerica.org/blog/?p=1561

Dunbar, Cynthia. "Article IV, Section 1 of the United States Constitution," May 10, 2011, http://www.constitutingamerica.org/blog/?p=1367

Duncan, William C. "Article I, Section 2, Clause 4 of the United States Constitution," February 25, 2011, http://www.constitutingamerica.org/blog/?p=723

___. "Article I, Section 5, Clause 1 of the United States Constitution," March 8, 2011, http://www.constitutingamerica.org/blog/?p=790

___. "Article I, Section 6, Clause 1 of the United States Constitution," March 11, 2011, http://www.constitutingamerica.org/blog/?p=841

___. "Article I, Section 8, Clause 17 of the United States Constitution," March 31, 2011, http://www.constitutingamerica.org/blog/?p=1005

___. "Article II, Section 1, Clause 7 of the United States Constitution," April 22, 2011, http://www.constitutingamerica.org/blog/?p=1224

___. "Amendment XX of the United States Constitution," June 15, 2011, http://www.constitutingamerica.org/blog/?p=1575

___. "Amendment XXV of the United States Constitution," June 22, 2011, http://www.constitutingamerica.org/blog/?p=1619

Faulkner, Scot. "Article I, Section 5, Clauses 3 & 4 of the United States Constitution," March 10, 2011, http://www.constitutingamerica.org/blog/?p=827

Hanna, Colin. "Amendment XV of the United States Constitution," June 8, 2011, http://www.constitutingamerica.org/blog/?p=1538

Hayward, Allison. "Article I, Section 8, Clause 7-8 of the United States Constitution," March 25, 2011, http://www.constitutingamerica.org/blog/?p=952

___. "Article I, Section 9, Clause 4-6 of the United States Constitution," April 6, 2011, http://www.constitutingamerica.org/blog/?p=1098

Heath, Hadley. "Amendment XIII of the United States Constitution," June 6, 2011, http://www.constitutingamerica.org/blog/?p=1518

Kickler, Troy PhD. "Article I, Section 8, Clauses 5-6 of the United States Constitution," March 24, 2011, http://www.constitutingamerica.org/blog/?p=948

Knipprath, Joerg W. "Article I, Section 4, Clauses 1-2 of the United States Constitution," March 7, 2011, http://www.constitutingamerica.org/blog/?p=748

___. "Article I, Section 7, Clause 1 of the United States Constitution," March 15, 2011, http://www.constitutingamerica.org/blog/?p=887

___. "Article I, Section 8, Clause 2 of the United States Constitution," March 21, 2011, http://www.constitutingamerica.org/blog/?p=923

___. "Article I, Section 8, Clause 18 of the United States Constitution," April 1, 2011, http://www.constitutingamerica.org/blog/?p=1011

___. "Article I, Section 9, Clause 2 and 3 of the United States Constitution," April 5, 2011, http://www.constitutingamerica.org/blog/?p=1086

___. "Article I, Section 10, Clause 1 of the United States Constitution," April 11, 2011, http://www.constitutingamerica.org/blog/?p=1155

___. "Article II, Section 1, Clause 3 of the United States Constitution," April 18, 2011, http://www.constitutingamerica.org/blog/?p=1193

___. "Article II, Section 1, Clause 8 of the United States Constitution," April 25, 2011, http://www.constitutingamerica.org/blog/?p=1246

___. "Article II, Section 2, Clause 3 of the United States Constitution," April 28, 2011, http://www.constitutingamerica.org/blog/?p=1280

___. "Article III, Section 2, Clause 1 of the United States Constitution," May 4, 2011, http://www.constitutingamerica.org/blog/?p=1314

___. "Article IV, Section 2 of the United States Constitution," May 11, 2011, http://www.constitutingamerica.org/blog/?p=1374

___. "Article V of the United States Constitution," May 16, 2011, http://www.constitutingamerica.org/blog/?p=1395

___. "Amendment VIII of the United States Constitution," May 30, 2011, http://www.constitutingamerica.org/blog/?p=1477

___. "Amendment XII of the United States Constitution," *Analyzing the Constitution in 90 Days*. Constituting America, June 3, 2011, http://www.constitutingamerica.org/blog/?p=1509

___. "Amendment XVIII of the United States Constitution," June 13, 2011, http://www.constitutingamerica.org/blog/?p=1557

___. "Amendment XXIV of the United States Constitution," June 21, 2011, http://www.constitutingamerica.org/blog/?p=1610

Kopel, David B. "Amendment II of the United States Constitution," May 20, 2011, http://www.constitutingamerica.org/blog/?p=1418

Lampkin, Marc S. "Amendment VI of the United States Constitution," May 26, 2011, http://www.constitutingamerica.org/blog/?p=1452

___. "Amendment XXII of the United States Constitution," June 17, 2011, http://www.constitutingamerica.org/blog/?p=1584

Langer, Andrew. "Article I, Section 3, Clause 3 of the United States Constitution," March 2, 2011, http://www.constitutingamerica.org/blog/?p=736

___. "Amendment V of the United States Constitution," May 25, 2011, http://www.constitutingamerica.org/blog/?p=1443

___. "Amendment X of the United States Constitution," June 1, 2011, http://www.constitutingamerica.org/blog/?p=1492

___. "Amendment XXI of the United States Constitution," June 16, 2011, http://www.constitutingamerica.org/blog/?p=1579

___. "Amendment XXVI of the United States Constitution," June 23, 2011, http://www.constitutingamerica.org/blog/?p=1625

McCaleb, Gary S. "Article II, Section 1, Clause 4 of the United States Constitution," April 19, 2011, http://www.constitutingamerica.org/blog/?p=1205

Morenoff, Dan, "Article I, Section 9, Clause 7 of the United States Constitution," April 7, 2011, http://www.constitutingamerica.org/blog/?p=1144

___. "Article IV, Section 3 of the United States Constitution," May 12, 2011, http://www.constitutingamerica.org/blog/?p=1378

___. "Article VII of the United States Constitution," May 18, 2011, http://www.constitutingamerica.org/blog/?p=1406

Morrisey, William, PhD. "Article I, Section 2, Clause 5 and Section 3, Clause 1 of the United States Constitution," February 28, 2011, http://www.constitutingamerica.org/blog/?p=728

___. "Article II, Section 2, Clause 2 of the United States Constitution," April 27, 2011, http://www.constitutingamerica.org/blog/?p=1274

___. "Article IV, Section 4 of the United States Constitution," May 13, 2011, http://www.constitutingamerica.org/blog/?p=1388

Postell, Joseph, PhD. "Article I, Section 3, Clause 2 of the United States Constitution," March 1, 2011, http://www.constitutingamerica.org/blog/?p=732

___. "Article II, Section 1, Clause 6 of the United States Constitution," April 21, 2011, http://www.constitutingamerica.org/blog/?p=1214

Reed, Jeffrey, "Amendment IV of the United States Constitution," May 24, 2011, http://www.constitutingamerica.org/blog/?p=1439

Rice, Charles E. J.S.D. "Article III, Section 2, Clause 2 of the United States Constitution," May 5, 2011, http://www.constitutingamerica.org/blog/?p=1317

Rogan, James E. "Article I, Section 3, Clause 6-7 of the United States Constitution," March 4, 2011, http://www.constitutingamerica.org/blog/?p=745

Ross, Tara. "Article II, Section 1, Clause 2 of the United States Constitution," April 15, 2011, http://www.constitutingamerica.org/blog/?p=1188

Rowley, Charles K., PhD. "Article 1, Section 1 of the United States Constitution," February 22, 2011, http://www.constitutingamerica.org/blog/?p=712

Rowley, Charles K., PhD. "Article I, Section 8, Clause 9 of the United States Constitution," March 28, 2011, http://www.constitutingamerica.org/blog/?p=962

___. "Article II, Section 3, Clause 1 of the United States Constitution," April 29, 2011, http://www.constitutingamerica.org/blog/?p=1284

___. "Amendment XXVII of the United States Constitution," June 24, 2011, http://www.constitutingamerica.org/blog/?p=1629

Scott, Kyle PhD. "Article I, Section 7, Clause 3 of the United

States Constitution," March 17, 2011, http://www
.constitutingamerica.org/blog/?p=909

___. "Article I, Section 9, Clause 8 of the United States Con-
stitution," April 8, 2011, http://www.constitutingamerica
.org/blog/?p=1151

___. "Article III, Section 1 of the United States Constitu-
tion," May 3, 2011, http://www.constitutingamerica.org/
blog/?p=1294

___. "Article III, Section 2, Clause 3 of the United States Con-
stitution," May 6, 2011, http://www.constitutingamerica
.org/blog/?p=1327

Schrader, George. "Article I, Section 7, Clause 2 of the
United States Constitution," March 16, 2011, http://www
.constitutingamerica.org/blog/?p=895

___. "Article I, Section 8, Clause 14-16 of the United
States Constitution," March 30, 2011, http://www
.constitutingamerica.org/blog/?p=1000

Shackelford, Kelly & Butterfield, Justin. "Amendment I of the
United States Constitution," May 19, 2011, http://www
.constitutingamerica.org/blog/?p=1412

Shaw, Julia. "Article I, Section 10, Clause 3 of the United
States Constitution," April 13, 2011, http://www
.constitutingamerica.org/blog/?p=1178

___. "Article II, Section 4 of the United States Constitu-
tion," May 2, 2011,http://www.constitutingamerica.org/
blog/?p=1291

Spiwak, Lawrence J. "Article II, Section 1, Clause 1 of the
United States Constitution," April 14, 2011, http://www
.constitutingamerica.org/blog/?p=1183

Stedman, W. David & Lewis. LaVaughn G. "Amendment VII
of the United States Constitution," May 27, 2011, http://
www.constitutingamerica.org/blog/?p=1461

Stewart, Nathaniel. "Article VI of the United States Constitution," May 17, 2011, http://www.constitutingamerica.org/
blog/?p=1402

Teller, Paul S. PhD. "Article I, Section 5, Clause 2 of the
United States Constitution," March 9, 2011, http://www
.constitutingamerica.org/blog/?p=821

Theriot, Kevin. "Amendment XI of the United States Constitution," June 2, 2011, http://www.constitutingamerica.org/
blog/?p=1504

___. "Amendment XIV of the United States Constitution," June
7, 2011, http://www.constitutingamerica.org/blog/?p=1532

Books

Amheim, Michael, Dr. *U.S. Constitution for Dummies* (Hobo-
ken: Wiley Publishing Inc., 2009).

Bailyn, Bernard, Editor. *Debate on the Constitution Part One*
(New York: Library Classics of the United States, Inc., 1993).

Cheney, Lynne. *We the People: the Story of Our Constitution*
(New York: Simon & Schuster Books for Young Readers,
2008).

Editors. Merriam-Webster's Collegiate Dictionary Eleventh
Edition (Springfield, Merriam-Webster, Inc., 2003).

Fritz, Jean *Shh! We're Writing the Constitution* (New York:
Puffin, 1997).

Levy, Elizabeth. If You Were There When They Signed the
Constitution (New York: Scholastic, 1992).

Madison, James, Alexander Hamilton, John Jay. The Federalist
Papers: America's Greatest Living Documents (Simi Valley,
NMD Books, 2010).

Articles and Web Sites

Barrett, Dan, "Intellectual Roots of Wall St. Protest Lie in
Academe." The Chronicle of Higher Education. October
16, 2011. http://chronicle.com/article/Intellectual-Roots-of
-Wall/129428/. Accessed April 24, 2012.

Congress for Kids Editorial Team, "Elections, the Electoral
College," *The Dirksen Congressional Center*, 2008., http://
www.congressforkids.net/Elections_electoralcollege
.htm (accessed April 12, 2012).

Editors, "The Founders' Constitution," Volume 4, Article 4,
Section 1, Document 4, The University of Chicago Press,
1987. http://presspubs.uchicago.edu/founders/documents/
a4_1s4.html, accessed April 12, 2012

Editors, "Constitution Quotes," Liberty-Tree Quotes and
Quotations, 1998-2012, http://quotes.libertytree.ca/quotes.
nsf/quotes_about!ReadForm&Count=50&Start=351&Res
trictToCategory=constitution (accessed April 27, 2012).

Editors, "The Madison Debates," the Avalon Project, Documents in Law, History, and Diplomacy, Yale Law School,
Lillian Goldman Law Library, 2008, http://avalon.law.yale.
edu/18th_century/debates_529.asp, (accessed April 27,
2012).

EDSITEment! Editorial Team, "The Constitutional Convention: What the Founding Fathers Said," National Endowment for the Humanities, 26 July 2010. http://edsitement.
neh.gov/ (accessed April 11, 2012).

Groves, Robert M., Dr., Thomas L. Mesenbourg, Arnold Jackson. "Strength in Numbers Your Guide to the 2010 Census.
Redistricting," *Data from the U.S. Census Bureau*. July 2010.,
http://www.census.gov/rdo/pdf/StrengthInNumbers2010.
pdf , (accessed April 27, 2010).

Mount, Steve. "Misspellings in the U.S. Constitution." *US
Constitution.net*. December 3, 2001, http://www.usconsti-
tution.net/constmiss.html, (accessed April 27, 2012).

Preston, Jennifer, "Journalists Cull Questions for Obama's
'Twitter Town Hall,'" *Media Decoder Behind the Screens,
Between the Lines, New York Times*, July 6, 2011.
http://mediadecoder.blogs.nytimes.com/2011/07/06/
journalists-cull-questions-for-obamas-twitter-
townhall/?scp=1&sq=obama's%20town%20hall&st=cse
(accessed April 12, 2012).

Peppitone, Julianne, "SOPA Explained: What it is and why
it Matters," CNN MoneyTech, January 20, 2012, http://
money.cnn.com/2012/01/17/technology/sopa_explained/
index.htm, accessed April 24, 2012.

Shmoop Editorial Team. "The Constitution," *Shmoop University, Inc.*, November 11, 2008, http://www.shmoop.com/
constitution/12th-amendment.html (accessed April 12,
2012).

Shmoop Editorial Team. "The Judiciary of the Articles of Confederation" *Shmoop University, Inc.* 11 November 2008.
http://www.shmoop.com/judicial-branch/articles-of-con-
federation-judiciary.html (accessed April 12, 2012).